Power Words Copymasters
A Bridge to Reading

McDougal Littell

BRIDGES TO
LITERATURE

LEVEL III

by
William McBride, Ph.D.

McDougal Littell
A HOUGHTON MIFFLIN COMPANY
Evanston, Illinois • Boston • Dallas

Table of Contents

Vocabulary Instruction for Older Students
by William McBride, Ph.D.

Teachers in middle and high schools today are faced with a number of students who are unable to read their textbooks. One way teachers can help their students improve reading comprehension is through direct vocabulary instruction. Comprehension is an active process in which students connect what they already know to information in a text. Research in the past decade has shown that direct vocabulary instruction has a significant effect on improving comprehension (Laflamme, 1997). This instructional workbook is designed to provide classroom teachers with the tools they need to help students become better readers through vocabulary development.

What Works

A number of strategies have been proven to be effective in helping students decode or understand words in texts (Blachowicz, C. & Lee, John, 1991; Ivey, G. & Broaddus, K., 1999; Moats, 2001; Stahl, S., 1999, Vacca & Vacca, 1993). Researchers recommend that teachers use the following strategies:
- Extensive reading at a child's independent reading level
- Instruction in the sound-symbol relationships in words (phonics)
- Instruction in word meanings
- Instruction in using context to derive meaning
- Instruction in morphology (roots, prefixes, and suffixes)
- Instruction in idiomatic expressions
- Practice in fluent reading
- Fun, interactive activities

Lesson Development

Power Words: A Bridge to Reading is designed to provide the types of instruction that are cited in the above research. The program has three levels. Each level is divided into twelve units. Each unit has three lessons and a unit test. The lessons are structured in the following format:

1. **Prior Knowledge/Oral Language:** Lessons begin by accessing students' prior knowledge. Students are prompted to share what they may already know about the lesson's target words. In some cases target words have multiple meanings. To help students understand multiple meanings, draw out as many meanings of a word as students are able to produce. For example, one student may define the word *current* as a noun (the current in the river) while another defines it as an adjective (a current newspaper).

2. **Power Words List:** Lessons 1 and 2 each introduce twelve target words to students. Lesson 3 reviews and reteaches the twenty-four words from the previous two lessons. The criteria for selecting target words in each lesson are as follows:
- Words that exemplify the particular skills being taught
- Words that are commonly found on standardized tests
- Words that are taught in McDougal Littell's *Bridges to Literature* program

3. **Instruction and Exercises:** Each lesson in a unit provides instruction and practice with <u>three</u> different skills. For example, Lesson 1 may cover synonyms, Latin and Greek roots, and context clues. One page of instruction and practice is devoted to each skill. Brain-based teaching methods reinforce the need for reteaching of concepts (Jensen, 1998; Sprenger, 1999). Consequently, Lesson 2 reteaches the same skills covered in Lesson 1, but with a new group of twelve target words. Finally, because students need multiple opportunities to learn how words are conceptually related (Vacca & Vacca, 1993), Lesson 3 reviews the previously taught twenty-four target words and, for a third time, reteaches the three skills covered in the unit.

4. **Skill Instruction:** The following skills are taught in every level of *Power Words: A Bridge to Reading*. Please note that most of these skills are covered multiple times within any one level. For example, in Level 1, affixes are covered in three separate units and context clues are covered in six separate units. The order of skill instruction for each level matches the skill instruction in McDougal Littell's *Bridges to Literature*.
   - Affixes
   - Compound Words
   - Multiple Meaning Words
   - Greek and Latin Roots
   - Context Clues
   - Shades of Meaning
   - Synonyms and Antonyms
   - Syllabication (through phonics)
   - Structural Analysis
   - Idioms
   - Homophones
   - Specialized Vocabulary
   - Foreign Words
   - Using a Dictionary

5. **Fluency:** Reading fluency is the ability to automatically recognize words. Fluency involves both decoding and comprehension skills. A fluent reader decodes so effortlessly that he or she can concentrate on meaning. Thus a good reader reads more quickly than a less-able reader. Readers can increase their fluency through practice. Consequently, in either Lesson 2 or 3 of every unit an exercise is devoted to fluency. Teachers can group students in pairs and have them practice reading to each other in "two-foot voices." Students can time each other and note errors, working towards correct, smooth readings.

6. **Unit Tests:** Each unit ends with a three-page test to evaluate students' knowledge of the target words and skills taught. The Unit Tests are designed to look like the test items on major standardized tests used in this country. Many items on standardized tests are written in formats that students do not see in normal reading tests. By exposing students to these formats, students are able to practice their test-taking skills.

7. **Answer Keys:** In the back of each level you will find Answer Keys for both the Lessons and the Unit Tests. For your information, a copy of the Dolch Basic Sight Word List has also been included. Students must know these words automatically to become fluent readers.

Instructional Plan for *Power Words*

You may want to follow the instructional plan described below.

Week 1 - Monday – Incorporate a highly-successful activity called Word Wall (Cunningham, P. 2000). Either write the twelve words from *Power Words* Lesson 1 on the board or cut out large construction paper "bricks" and put the words on the wall. At the start of class, ask students to number a sheet of paper from one to twelve. As an oral activity, call out the first word and ask if anyone in the class knows its meaning and how he or she knows it. If no one knows the word, use the word in a sentence that provides enough context so that students can discern its definition. Come to a group decision as to the best definition of the word, write the definition on the board and have students copy it down. You may have one student look up the word in a dictionary, select the definition that fits the way the word is used in the sentence, and read the definition aloud. Continue until all twelve words are defined. Spend the rest of the period with regular activities. If you are using McDougal Littell's high interest/low readability series *Bridges to Literature*, begin the first selection in the unit.

Tuesday – Begin the class with Word Wall by calling out the definitions from Monday and have students copy the correct word from the wall. In this way, students are practicing the correct spellings while learning the definitions. Pass out *Power Words* Lesson 1 Worksheets and guide students through the three pages of activities to make sure they understand the format of each exercise. If time allows, continue with regular literature-based activities. In *Bridges*, use the SkillBuilder sheets related to the selection you read the day before.

Wednesday – Begin the class with Word Wall by calling out the definitions. Then review the answers to the Lesson 1 exercises. Finish class with your regular literature-based activities. In *Bridges*, finish the first selection and move to the second.

Thursday – Before students arrive, add the twelve words from *Power Words* Lesson 2 to your Word Wall. Follow Monday's procedure of having students define the new words and copy the definitions. Continue with your regular activities. In *Bridges*, finish the second selection and any Skillbuilder worksheets.

Friday – Begin the class with Word Wall, calling out the definitions of ALL twenty-four words as the students write the correct word. Finish the class with regular literature-based activities or move to the third story in *Bridges*.

Week 2 - Monday – Begin the class with Word Wall, calling out all twenty-four words from the previous week. Then distribute *Power Words* Lesson 2 Worksheets. Guide students through the activities. Students should be able to work more independently on these lessons as these skills are the same skills taught in Lesson 1.

Tuesday – Begin the class with Word Wall with all twenty-four words. Review the answers to the Lesson 2 Worksheets. Finish the class with regular literature-based activities. In *Bridges*, move into the fourth selection if applicable or finish any activities from previous selections covered.

Wednesday – Begin the class with Word Wall with all twenty-four words. Pass out *Power Words* Lesson 3 Worksheets, which reviews the skills and words taught in the first two lessons. Guide students through these activities. Allow students to take Lesson 3 home to study with an adult in the home. Finish the class with regular literature-based activities. In *Bridges*, finish covering the literature and SkillBuilder sheets in the unit. Tell students to study their *Power Words* for a test on Friday.

Thursday – Begin the class with Word Wall with all twenty-four words. Review the answers to the Lesson 3 Worksheets. Finish the class with regular literature-based activities.

Friday – Pass out the *Power Words* Unit Test. Because parts of the test resemble test items on major standardized tests, you may want to explain variations in format for certain test items. Count the test as a major grade and place it in the student's portfolio.

Bibliography

Billmeyer, R. & Barton, M. (1998). *Teaching Reading in the Content Areas: If Not Me, Then Who?* Aurora, CO: McREL.

Blachowicz, C., & Lee, J. (November, 1991). Vocabulary development in the whole literacy classroom. *The Reading Teacher, 45 (3), 188–194.*

Cunningham, P. (2000). *Phonics They Use: Words for Reading and Writing* (3rd ed.) New York: Longman.

Ivey, G., & Broaddus, K. (1991). 1700+ students speak out about middle school reading. Paper presented at the 49th annual meeting of the National Reading Conference, Orlando, FL.

Jensen, Eric. (1998). *Teaching with the Brain in Mind.* Alexandria, VA: ASCD.

Laflamme, J.G. (1997). The effect of the Multiple Exposure Vocabulary Method and the Target Reading/Writing Strategy on test scores. *Journal of Adolescent and Adult Literacy, 40 (5), 372–381.*

Micklos, J. & Freeman, M. (Eds.). (Aug./Sept., 2002) Examining Evidence: New IRA position statement on evidence-based reading instruction lists practices proven effective by valid research. *Reading Today 20 (1).*

Moats, Louisa C., (March, 2001). When Older Students Can't Read. *Educational Leadership.* (pp. 36–40) Alexandria, VA: ASCD.

Sprenger, Marilee. (1999). *Learning and Memory: The Brain in Action.* Alexandria, VA: ASCD.

Stahl, S. (1986). Three principles of effective vocabulary instruction. *Journal of Reading, 29, 662–671.*

Stahl, S. (Stahl, Steven. (1999). *Vocabulary Development.* Cambridge, MA: Brookline Books.

Vacca, R.T., & Vacca, J.L. (1993). Content Area Reading (4th ed.). New York: Harper Collins.

Power Words

Look at the words below. Circle any that you think you may know. Be ready to tell the class what the word means. Also tell the class how you think you know that word.

anxiety	dull	hearty	obligation
broke	extravagant	lie	pastry
chef	film	light	point

Part 1: Multiple-Meaning Words

The word *multiple* means many. **Multiple-meaning words** are words that have more than one meaning. For example, the word *slide* can mean a thing children play on in a playground. It can also mean to run and throw oneself down on the ground, as to slide into home plate in baseball.

A. Read each sentence below. Think about how the **bold word** in the sentence is used. Then read the two different meanings of that word below. Write the letter of the definition in the blank that matches the meaning of the bold word in the sentence.

_____1. Every morning the evil eye had a blue **film** over it.
  a. a thin milky-colored covering
  b. a movie

_____2. The young man kept making the **point** that he wasn't mad.
  a. a sharp end
  b. a main idea

_____3. The lantern was covered so it showed no **light**.
  a. not heavy
  b. brightness

_____4. As the day **broke**, the young man started fixing breakfast.
  a. began
  b. without any money

_____5. The old man was so frightened that he wouldn't **lie** down.
  a. to speak an untruth
  b. to stretch out in a horizontal position

_____6. The eye always had a **dull** blue color.
  a. stupid
  b. not a bright color

Name _____ Date _____

Part 2: Idioms

An **idiom** is a statement or phrase that doesn't mean exactly what the words say. People in different places have different ways of saying things. For example, to say that a person "has a green thumb" does not mean that his thumb is the color green. It means that this person is able to grow plants very easily. "Has a green thumb" is an idiom.

A. See if you can match the idioms in the left column with the meanings in the right.

Idiom	Meaning
_____ under the weather	a. show up unexpectedly
_____ drop in	b. get it exactly right
_____ hit the nail on the head	c. feeling sick
_____ hightail it	d. leave in a hurry

B. Each sentence below has an underlined idiom. Use the words around the idiom to help you figure out what the idiom means. Then read the list of definitions below. Write the letter of the definition that matches the idiom in the line behind the sentence.

A. someone very important	F. to keep in contact
B. chosen	G. to be quiet but strong
C. someone who is stupid	H. always drive fast
D. got too scared to do something	I. very slow
E. try something without any preparation	J. to bother or annoy

1. I had never cooked, but my dad said to get in the kitchen and <u>sink or swim</u>. _____

2. David acted like a <u>big shot</u> when he got his promotion at work. _____

3. Sarah did stupid things all the time; she's a real <u>birdbrain</u>. _____

4. My dad is a real <u>lead foot</u>. He drives fast all the time. _____

5. I wanted to ask Maria out, but I got <u>cold feet</u> and didn't call. _____

6. Until Larry loses some weight, he'll always be <u>slow as molasses in winter</u>. _____

7. Once you move I hope you'll still <u>stay in touch</u>. _____

8. Boy, does that new student <u>bug me</u>! _____

9. Don't let Jamie fool you because he's quiet. He might <u>walk softly but carries a bigstick</u>. _____

10. Juanita <u>got the nod</u> to play point guard on the basketball team. _____

Part 3: Context Clues

The words or phrases that surround an unknown word are called **context clues**. Sometimes you can figure out the meaning of an unknown word from the words that appear near by. For example, see how the other words in the sentence below tell you that *extravagant* means high-priced.

I couldn't afford such an extravagant coat. I didn't need something so expensive.

A. Use context clues to figure out the meaning of the **bold** word. Darken in the circle with the correct definition that makes the most sense.

1. The lady who cooked the turnovers was quite a **chef**.
   - teacher
   - sales woman
   - cook
   - waitress

2. The boy had great **anxiety** when he thought he had been caught lying.
   - excitement
   - worry
   - sadness
   - chills

3. Fausto had an **obligation** to return the twenty dollar bill.
   - duty
   - idea
   - choice
   - bet

4. The turnover was a delicious **pastry** filled with sugar and apples.
   - orange
   - hot dog
   - baked dessert
   - funny

5. The smiling man gave Fausto a **hearty** greeting when he arrived at the door.
   - sad
   - questionable
   - curious
   - warm

Power Words

Look at the words below. Circle any that you think you may know. Be ready to tell the class what the word means. Also tell the class how you think you know that word.

confided	loaf	novelty	rich
fatigued	mass	profile	tracks
involved	morsel	raked	yard

Part 1: Multiple-Meaning Words

Multiple-meaning words are words that have more than one meaning. For example, the word *play* can mean to have fun. It can also be a dramatic show you watch in a theater.

A. Read each sentence below. Think about how the **bold word** is used in the sentence. Then read the two different meanings of that word below. Write the letter of the definition in the blank that matches the meaning of the bold word in the sentence.

_____1. The doughnuts were cream-filled and very **rich**.
   a. wealthy
   b. having large amounts of choice ingredients, such as butter and sugar

_____2. Steve refused to work and would sit and **loaf** all day.
   a. to do nothing
   b. a shaped mass of food

_____3. The battleship **raked** the other boat with cannons.
   a. to aim heavy gunfire along the length of an object
   b. to scratch or scrape

_____4. We sold a number of old things at our **yard** sale.
   a. the area of ground surrounding a building
   b. a measurement totaling three feet long

_____5. Our family always went to **mass** on Friday evening.
   a. a group of separate parts joined together or unified
   b. a religious service in the Catholic church

_____6. My mother's voice stopped me in my **tracks**.
   a. steps
   b. metal rails on which trains run

_____7. The photo showed the young girl's **profile**.
   a. side view of a face
   b. a written description of someone

Unit 1, Lesson 2

Part 2: Idioms

An **idiom** is a statement or phrase that doesn't mean exactly what the words say. For example, to say that a person is "up a tree" may not mean that he has climbed a tree. It may mean that he is in a very bad situation. "Up a tree" is an idiom.

A. Each sentence below has an underlined idiom. Use the words around the idiom to help you figure out what the idiom means. Then read the list of definitions below. Write the letter of the definition that matches the idiom in the line behind the sentence.

A. feeling great
B. learn to do well
C. clumsy
D. work very hard
E. listen
F. disappeared

G. more energy
H. sad
I. very occupied
J. lose one's temper, get angry
K. try not to smile
L. passed or finished

1. <u>Give me your ear</u> because I have something important to tell you. _____

2. Shaq had been <u>busy as a bee</u> keeping the other team from scoring. _____

3. It was hard to <u>keep a straight face</u> when Luis fell out of his chair. _____

4. I've been very <u>blue</u> since my girlfriend broke up with me. _____

5. I needed a <u>second wind</u> when the game went long into overtime. _____

6. Sheila felt better about her job once she got the first week <u>under her belt</u>. _____

7. Lorrie was <u>walking on air</u> when the cute guy asked her out on a date. _____

8. Some people never <u>get the hang</u> of surfing and fall down often. _____

9. My father said he would <u>blow his stack</u> if I didn't clean up my room. _____

10. Our new plans for the show just went <u>up in smoke</u>. _____

11. If you don't <u>put your nose to the grindstone</u> you won't get anything finished.

_____

12. Fausto was <u>all thumbs</u> when he first started playing the guitar. _____

Unit 1, Lesson 2

Part 3: Context Clues

The words or phrases that surround an unknown word are called **context clues**. Sometimes you can figure out the meaning of an unknown word from the words that appear near by. For example, see how the other words in the sentence below tell you that kingpin means "the most important or powerful person."

My dad is the kingpin where he works. Everyone else obeys his orders.

A. Use context clues to figure out the meaning of the **bold** word. Darken in the circle with the correct definition that makes the most sense.

1. David was very **fatigued** after the race. He didn't have the energy to walk home.
   - ○ happy
   - ○ excited
   - ○ bored
   - ○ tired

2. With guilt, my sister **confided** to me that she had stolen the brownies.
   - ○ lied
   - ○ spoke
   - ○ told in secret
   - ○ remembered

3. The dog was given only a **morsel** of food, and he was still hungry
   - ○ small piece
   - ○ bone
   - ○ choice
   - ○ second helping

4. During the rainy winter, it is a **novelty** to have a week of sunshine.
   - ○ regular happening
   - ○ reason
   - ○ chance
   - ○ new or unusual happening

5. I would try to explain the argument to you but it is really difficult and **involved**.
   - ○ sad
   - ○ complex
   - ○ silly
   - ○ easy

Power Words Review

Look at the words below. Circle any that you think you may know. Be ready to tell the class what the word means. Also tell the class how you think you know that word.

anxiety	fatigued	loaf	point
broke	film	mass	profile
chef	hearty	morsel	raked
confided	involved	novelty	rich
dull	lie	obligation	tracks
extravagant	light	pastry	yard

Part 1: Multiple-Meaning Words

Multiple-meaning words are words that have more than one meaning. For example, the word *watch* can mean to observe something. It is also a thing that tells time.

A. Read each sentence below. Think about how the **bold word** is used in the sentence. Then read the two different meanings of that word below. Write the letter of the definition in the blank that matches the meaning of the bold word in the sentence.

_____1. There was a **mass** of people at the dance.
    a. a group of separate parts joined together or unified
    b. a religious service in the Catholic church

_____2. Fausto **raked** the leaves from the neighbor's yard..
    a. to aim heavy gunfire along the length of an object
    b. to scratch or scrape

_____3. I wrote a **profile** of Abraham Lincoln for History class.
    a. side view of a face
    b. a written description of someone

_____4. After two hours shopping at the mall, Judy was **broke** when she left.
    a. began
    b. without any money

_____5. On Fridays my parents love to go out to a **film**.
    a. a movie
    b. a thin milky-colored covering

_____6. I'm a good student in English class but I'm pretty **dull** at math.
    a. stupid
    b. not a bright color

Unit 1, Lesson 3

Part 2: Idioms

An **idiom** is a statement or phrase that doesn't mean exactly what the words say. For example, to say "get the lead out" doesn't mean to take away the metal called lead. It means to hurry up. "Get the lead out" is an idiom.

A. Below are each of the idioms you have studied before. Match the idiom with its definition by writing the letter of the definition by the correct idiom.

_____	1. keep a straight face	A. clumsy
_____	2. stay in touch	B. feeling sick
_____	3. blow his/her stack	C. chosen
_____	4. walking on air	D. feeling great
_____	5. big shot	E. someone very important
_____	6. got the nod	F. keep in contact with
_____	7. all thumbs	G. show up unexpectedly
_____	8. under the weather	H. work very hard
_____	9. drop in	I. get very angry; lose one's temper
_____	10. put your nose to the grindstone	J. try not to smile

B. Fluency: Practice reading the paragraph below until you can read it smoothly. There are 13 idioms in the paragraph. Circle each one as you find it.

Maria is always bugging me. She is such a birdbrain. She will walk up to me in the school hallway and say, "Hey, give me your ear a second." I don't just walk away. I hightail it! As I'm running she yells, "Stay in touch."

She always has a lot of stuff going on. She prides herself on being busy as a bee. After a few minutes with her, I feel like I need a second wind. She really tires me out. I think her parents must tell her every morning to put her nose to the grindstone.

Her latest hobby is skateboarding. At first she was all thumbs. Maria said she decided to buy a skateboard with no lessons and either sink or swim. Eventually she got the hang of it. Now when she is flying down the sidewalk, she says it makes her feel like she's walking on air. Personally, I have trouble keeping a straight face.

Unit 1, Lesson 3

Part 3: Context Clues

Remember that the words or phrases that surround an unknown word are called **context clues**. These words may help you figure out the meaning of the unknown word.

A. Use context clues to figure out the meaning of the **bold** word. Darken in the circle with the correct definition that makes the most sense.

1. Mr. Thomas, our teacher, was rarely absent. It was a **novelty** having a substitute.
   - ○ regular happening
   - ○ chance
   - ○ new or unusual happening
   - ○ reason

2. My favorite **pastry** is one filled with sugar and cherries.
   - ○ soup
   - ○ day
   - ○ recipe
   - ○ baked dessert

3. I **confided** quietly to my brother that Jesse had broken his model airplane.
   - ○ told in secret
   - ○ spoke
   - ○ cried
   - ○ remembereed

4. Larry said he sweated with **anxiety** before he took the winning shot to end the game.
   - ○ chills
   - ○ intelligence
   - ○ worry or fear
   - ○ self-confidence

5. The four pages of instructions to run my new CD player are very **involved**.
   - ○ sad
   - ○ easy
   - ○ silly
   - ○ complicated or complex

6. Without any rain for the crops, the farmers feared there wouldn't be a **morsel** of food.
   - ○ choice
   - ○ small piece
   - ○ second dish
   - ○ bone

Part A: Multiple-Meaning Words

Directions: Read each sentence below. Find the word that fits in both sentences.

1. The evil eye had a thin, blue _____ covering it.

   We went to the cinema to watch the _____ .

   ○ eyelid
   ○ film
   ○ stars
   ○ show

2. The new ship will _____ the fort with its cannon.

   Every fall, Sarah goes out to _____ the front yard.

   ○ mow
   ○ sow
   ○ rake
   ○ plow

3. I was stopped in my _____ when I saw the ghost.

   The train left the _____ at the bend by the river.

   ○ shoes
   ○ station
   ○ hurry
   ○ tracks

4. When the day _____, the sun came streaming in.

   Tired of being _____, the man began to look for a job.

   ○ started
   ○ broke
   ○ poor
   ○ opened

5. The police asked for a _____ of the robber.

   I always show people my _____ when someone's going to take my picture.

   ○ profile
   ○ smile
   ○ clothes
   ○ jail

Part B: Idioms

Directions: Match the idiom in **Column A** with its meaning in **Column B**. Write the letter of the correct definition in the blank provided.

Column A

1. _____ big shot

2. _____ stay in touch

3. _____ under her belt

4. _____ blow his/her stack

5. _____ under the weather

6. _____ hightail it

7. _____ blue

8. _____ all thumbs

9. _____ birdbrain

10. _____ walking on air

11. _____ second wind

12. _____ sink or swim

13. _____ bug me

14. _____ up in smoke

15. _____ busy as a bee

Column B

A. to keep in contact with someone

B. to lose one's temper; get angry

C. clumsy

D. to bother or annoy

E. feeling great

F. work very hard

G. to try something without preparation

H. disappeared

I. leave in a hurry

J. feeling sick

K. someone who is stupid

L. to get more energy

M. passed; finished; or over with

N. sad

O. someone very important

Name _____   Date _____

Part C: Context Clues

Directions: For each numbered blank, there is a list of words with the same number. Choose the word from each list that best completes the meaning of the paragraph.

1. The _____ was angry at the customers. Not one had tasted a single _____
   (1)   (2)
   of food.

   1. ○ shopkeeper   **2.** ○ morsel
           ○ salesman   ○ choice
           ○ teacher   ○ spice
           ○ chef   ○ bone

2. My sister _____ to me. In a tired voice she admitted that after two weeks of
                (3)
   hard and constant travel she was _____.
                                        (4)

   3. ○ lied   **4.** ○ married
           ○ confided   ○ fatigued
           ○ yelled   ○ reading
           ○ remembered   ○ swimming

3. I had an _____ to eat the whole meal. My best friend's mother had spent days
            (5)
   cooking a meal as a _____ welcome.
                          (6)

   5. ○ anger   **6.** ○ hearty
           ○ idea   ○ evil
           ○ bet   ○ questionable
           ○ obligation   ○ sad

4. The decision to go to war is _____ and not a simple one. It causes great
                                   (7)
   _____ among the politicians who must decide.
      (8)

   7. ○ silly   **8.** ○ anxiety
           ○ easy   ○ love
           ○ involved   ○ cheer
           ○ fine   ○ sickness

Power Words

Look at the words below. Circle any that you think you may know. Be ready to tell the class what the word means. Also tell the class how you think you know that word.

antiaircraft   illiterate   incapable   malnourish

antisocial   immobile   infield   mound

illegal   immortal   malformed   shortstop

Part 1: Prefixes and Base Words

A **base word** is a word that can stand alone. A **prefix** is a word part added to the beginning of a base word. For example, in the word *imperfect*, perfect is the base word and *im-* is the prefix added at the beginning. Knowing the meaning of a prefix helps you figure out the meaning of the whole word. *Imperfect* means "not perfect." Study the meaning of the following prefixes until you can remember what each means.

in- or *im-* or *il-* means "not" / *anti-* means "against" / *mal-* means "bad"

A. Draw a line between the **base word** and the **prefix** for each word below. Then write what the word means on the line.

1. antifreeze - _____

2. incapable - _____

3. malformed - _____

4. antiaircraft - _____

5. illiterate - _____

6. immortal - _____

7. antiterrorism - _____

8. maltreat - _____

9. immobile - _____

10. antisocial - _____

11. illegal - _____

12. malnourish - _____

Part 2: Idioms

Remember that an **idiom** is a statement or phrase that doesn't mean exactly what the words say. For example, to say that a person "has a green thumb" does not mean that his thumb is the color green. It means that this person is able to grow plants very easily. "Has a green thumb" is an idiom.

A. See if you can match the idioms in the left column with the meanings in the right.

Idiom

_____ a big shot

_____ bug me

_____ got the nod

_____ lead foot

Meaning

a. chosen

b. someone very important

c. a fast driver

d. bother me

B. Each sentence below has an underlined idiom. Use the words around the idiom to help you figure out what the idiom means. Then read the list of definitions below. Write the letter of the definition that matches the idiom in the line following the sentence.

A. in the exact center

B. a wonderful thing to happen

C. beginning to do well

D. to get under something for safety

E. made one very afraid or horrified

F. not much chance of success

G. searched

H. to get the courage

I. completely dark

J. to understand right now

1. Look, <u>get this straight</u>, you do what I tell you to do. _____

2. The night was <u>black as pitch</u> and we could see nothing. _____

3. The players on our football team are really <u>coming into their own</u>. _____

4. Luis <u>combed</u> the riverbank for his lost fishing rod. _____

5. I <u>took cover</u> when the hail started falling. _____

6. When we got our new house, it was a <u>dream come true</u>. _____

7. The school's baseball team was so bad that <u>the odds were against them</u>. _____

8. It took Mark three days to <u>work up the nerve</u> to ask Julie out for a date. _____

9. The waiter fell <u>smack-dab</u> in the middle of the cake. _____

10. The book was so scary that <u>my blood ran cold</u>. _____

Unit 2, Lesson 1

Part 3: Specialized Vocabulary

People who work in a special field, such as sports or science, use special words. They use a **specialized vocabulary** to talk about their subjects. For example, a soccer player might use the word **goalie**. When you come across specialized vocabulary, look at the words and sentences around the special word to help you figure out its meaning.

A. The following sentences have specialized vocabulary about baseball. The specialized vocabulary is in **bold**. Underline the words in the sentence that tell you what each bold word means. Then write a definition on the line.

1. A team looks great as they run out onto the **diamond,** or baseball field, to face the other team.

   meaning: _____

2. Batters love to hit a **homer** and watch the baseball sail over the outfield fence.

   meaning: _____

3. A baseball field has two parts. The **infield** is the part without the grass near the batter.

   meaning: _____

4. Batters hate to swing and miss a pitch. They only get three of these **strikes**.

   meaning: _____

5. The **shortstop** has to be a very good player because many balls are hit between second and third base.

   meaning: _____

6. The batter stands at **home plate**, the spot in front of the catcher, facing the pitcher.

   meaning: _____

7. A ball that is hit up into the air is called a **fly ball**.

   meaning: _____

8. The pitcher throws the ball from a small hill known as the **mound**.

   meaning: _____

Power Words

Look at the words below. Circle any that you think you may know. Be ready to tell the class what the word means. Also tell the class how you think you know that word.

baton	hypertension	multilingual	orchestra
conductor	instrument	multiparty	percussion
hypercritic	monogamy	omnidirectional	reed

Part 1: Prefixes and Base Words

A **base word** is a word that can stand alone. A **prefix** is a word part added to the beginning of a base word. For example, in the word **multicolor**, **color** is the base word and **multi-** is the prefix added at the beginning. Knowing the meaning of a prefix helps you figure out the meaning of the whole word. *Multicolor* means "many colors." Study the meaning of the following prefixes until you can remember what each means.

hyper- means "more than normal" / *omni-* means "all"
mono- means "one" / *multi-* means "many"

A. Circle six words that begin with the prefixes **hyper, omni, mono,** and **multi** in the sentences below. Then write a definition for each word. Use a dictionary if necessary.

1. Our government as a multiparty system, Democrats, Republicans, and others.

   meaning: _____

2. My music teacher is such a hypercritic. She finds fault with everything I play.

   meaning: _____

3. Sheila believes in monogamy. She has a relationship with one person at a time.

   meaning: _____

4. The local radio station sends out signals that are omnidirectional.

   meaning: _____

5. Jose is so smart. He is multilingual, speaking both Spanish and English.

   meaning: _____

6. Marty takes pills for her hypertension. These keep her blood pressure down.

   meaning: _____

Unit 2, Lesson 2

Part 2: Idioms

Remember that an **idiom** is a statement or phrase that doesn't mean exactly what the words say. For example, to say that John is "under the weather" does not mean that he is standing in the rain. It means that he is feeling sick. "Under the weather" is an idiom.

A. Each sentence below has an underlined idiom. Use the words around the idiom to help you figure out what the idiom means. Then read the list of definitions below. Write the letter of the definition that matches the idiom in the line behind the sentence.

A. working very hard   H. the worst part of a fight
B. taking care of   I. caused large damage or problems
C. became very sad   J. begin to cry
D. stay in one place; not move   K. pay a high price
E. got involved with; befriended   L. slowly falling apart
F. hurt very much   M. told everyone
G. strongly doesn't want to do something   N. everywhere

1. When I see a hurt animal I just <u>go to pieces</u>. _____

2. My grandma told my mother that she loves <u>looking after</u> the children. _____

3. Sarah <u>fell in with</u> a bad group of students. _____

4. The mean store owner made us <u>pay a red price</u> for the candy. _____

5. The local farmers were really <u>bent to the task</u> at harvest time. _____

6. My mother told my little brother to not run around and <u>stay put</u>. _____

7. The tornado really <u>took its toll</u> on the town. _____

8. Gene's <u>heart sank</u> when Louisa refused to go to the dance. _____

9. The old car sitting in the field was just <u>wasting away</u>. _____

10. The airforce arrived <u>in the thick of battle</u> and saved our troops. _____

11. The bright sunlight in the desert <u>stabbed at his eyes</u>. _____

12. The principal <u>rang out the news</u> that our school had done well on our tests.

_____

13. David was <u>dead against</u> getting on the roller coaster. It scared him. _____

14. Mr. Davis searched <u>high and low</u> for his car keys but couldn't find them. _____

Unit 2, Lesson 2

Part 3: Specialized Vocabulary

People who work in a special activity or occupation, such as sports or science, use special words. They use a **specialized vocabulary** to talk about their subjects. For example, a doctor might use the word **operation**. When you come across specialized vocabulary, look at the words and sentences around the special word to help you figure out its meaning.

A. The following sentences have specialized vocabulary about music. The specialized vocabulary is in **bold**. Underline the words in the sentence that tell you what each bold word means. Then write a definition on the line. Use a dictionary if necessary.

1. The **conductor** led the musicians through some wonderful music.

   meaning: _____

2. Every expert musician knows how to play his or her **instrument** well.

   meaning: _____

3. The conductor waved her **baton**, showing us the speed with which to play.

   meaning: _____

4. There are many **string instruments**, such as violins, violas, and cellos.

   meaning: _____

5. Some **orchestras** have over one hundred musicians playing in large concert halls.

   meaning: _____

6. The **brass section** is made up of the trumpets, trombones, and French horns.

   meaning: _____

7. The saxophone uses a **reed** to make sound, which is a thin slice of bamboo that vibrates when the player blows on it.

   meaning: _____

8. My favorite part of the orchestra is the **percussion**, which is anything you beat on such as the drums, bells, and chimes.

   meaning: _____

Power Words Review

Look at the words below. Circle any that you think you may know. Be ready to tell the class what the word means. Also tell the class how you think you know that word.

antiaircraft	illegal	instrument	multiparty
antisocial	illiterate	malformed	omnidirectional
baton	immobile	malnourish	orchestra
conductor	immortal	monogamy	percussion
hypercritic	incapable	mound	reed
hypertension	infield	multilingual	shortstop

Part 1: Prefixes and Base Words

Remember that a **base word** is a word that can stand alone. A **prefix** is a word part added to the beginning of a base word. Knowing the meaning of a prefix helps you figure out the meaning of the whole word. Study the meaning of the following prefixes until you can remember what each means.

in- or *im-* or *il-* means "not" / *anti-* means "against" / *mal-* means "bad"
hyper- means "more than normal" / *omni-* means "all"
mono- means "one" / *multi-* means "many"

A. Draw a line between the base word and the prefix for each word below. Then write what the word means on the line.

1. hypercritical - _____

2. incapable - _____

3. malformed - _____

4. monogamy - _____

5. illiterate - _____

6. multilingual - _____

7. antiterrorism - _____

8. maltreat - _____

9. impossible - _____

10. omnidirectional - _____

Part 2: Idioms

Remember that an **idiom** is a statement or phrase that doesn't mean exactly what the words say. Use the ideas of the entire sentence and paragraph to figure out the real meaning of an idiom.

A. Below are each of the idioms you have studied before. Match the idiom with its definition by writing the letter of the definition by the correct idiom.

_____ 1. pay a red price	A. to get the courage
_____ 2. black as pitch	B. everywhere
_____ 3. dead against	C. completely dark
_____ 4. work up the nerve	D. searched for
_____ 5. wasting away	E. stay in one place; not move
_____ 6. took cover	F. pay a high price
_____ 7. high and low	G. to get under something for safety
_____ 8. bent to the task	H. work very hard
_____ 9. combed for	I. strongly doesn't want to do it
_____ 10. stay put	J. slowly falling apart

B. Fluency: Practice reading the paragraph below until you can read it smoothly. There are 15 idioms in the paragraph. Circle each one as you find it.

Our army company had been in the thick of battle for days. When the first shots were fired, we took cover. My heart sank at the constant sound of gunfire. The captain said, "Now, get this straight. I'm dead against us running away. We have already paid a red price in this battle. I know this war is taking its toll, but we have to fight."

That night there was no moon and it was black as pitch. We decided to work up our nerve and go look for the enemy. Our troops combed the woods for them. We searched high and low. We were sure they would stay put and fight. I was afraid if I saw an enemy soldier my blood would run cold with fear. But like a dream come true, we realized the enemy had run away first. We ran back to camp and rang out the news that the battle was over.

Unit 2, Lesson 3

Part 3: Specialized Vocabulary

People who work in a special activity or occupation, such as sports or science, use special words. They use a specialized vocabulary to talk about their subjects. When you come across specialized vocabulary, look at the words and sentences around the special word to help you figure out its meaning.

A. Look at the drawing of a baseball field below. Use the special vocabulary words below to label the parts.

diamond   fly ball   infield
mound   shortstop   homeplate

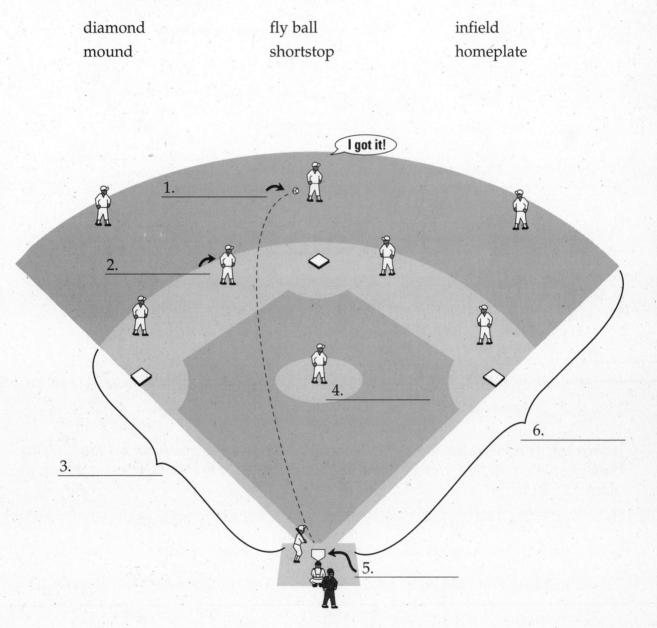

Part A: Prefixes and Base Words

Directions: Match the word in **Column A** with its definition in **Column B**. Write the letter of the correct definition in the blank provided.

Column A

1. _____ malformed
2. _____ multilingual
3. _____ illegal
4. _____ omnidirectional
5. _____ hypercritic
6. _____ maltreat
7. _____ antiaircraft
8. _____ immobile
9. _____ multiparty
10. _____ antiterrorism
11. _____ incapable
12. _____ antisocial
13. _____ malnourish
14. _____ antifreeze
15. _____ monogamy

Column B

A. having more than one political party

B. not lawful

C. to treat someone or something badly

D. not capable

E. a weapon designed to attack airplanes

F. eat a poor diet

G. a liquid that prevents engines from freezing

H. speaking many languages

I. unable to move

J. someone who doesn't like being with others

K. having a relationship with one person at a time

L. very critical

M. in all directions

N. against terrorist activities or persons

O. badly made or created

Directions: The following words have been divided both correctly and incorrectly into their prefixes and base words. Write the letter of the correctly divided word on the blank.

1. _____   A. hyper / critic   B. hyp / ercritic

2. _____   A. anti / social   B. an / tisocial

3. _____   A. il / legal   B. ill / egal

4. _____   A. om / nidirectional   B. omni / directional

5. _____   A. multi / party   B. mul / tiparty

Unit 2, Test

Part B: Idioms

Directions: Match the idiom in **Column A** with its meaning in **Column B**. Write the letter of the correct definition in the blank provided.

Column A

1. _____ dead against

2. _____ stay put

3. _____ bent to the task

4. _____ dream come true

5. _____ combed for

6. _____ work up the nerve

7. _____ took cover

8. _____ black as pitch

9. _____ heart sank

10. _____ wasting away

11. _____ high and low

12. _____ pay a red price

13. _____ took its toll

14. _____ looking after

15. _____ get this straight

Column B

A. very dark

B. get up the courage

C. stay in one place; not move

D. to get under something for safety

E. everywhere

F. taking care of

G. pay a high price

H. slowly falling apart

I. to understand right now

J. became very sad

K. searched for

L. working very hard

M. a wonderful thing to happen

N. caused large damage or problems

O. strongly doesn't want to do something

Unit 2, Test

Part C: Specialized Vocabulary

Directions: The words in the following list belong to one of the two specialized vocabulary groups at the bottom of the page. Write each word under its correct label.

diamond	infield	percussion
conductor	fly ball	string instruments
orchestra	mound	home plate
reed	baton	brass section
shortstop	homer	instrument
strikes		

Category A: Baseball

_____   _____   _____

_____   _____   _____

_____   _____

Category B: Music

_____   _____   _____

_____   _____   _____

_____   _____

Power Words

Look at the words below. Circle any that you think you may know. Be ready to tell the class what the word means. Also tell the class how you think you know that word.

annoy	disputes	repairman	sacred
custom	hilarity	required	system
disgusted	insults	roadblock	wistful

Part 1: Context Clues

Sometimes you can figure out the meaning of an unknown word from the words that appear near by. The words or phrases that surround an unknown word are called **context clues**. For example, see how the second sentence below tells you that *artificial* means fake.

> The plastic flowers looked so *artificial*. I just hate fake flowers.

A. Use context clues to figure out the meaning of the **bold** word. Darken in the circle with the correct definition.

1. Sam's mother had a **system** to always do things the same way.
   - ○ job
   - ○ reason
   - ○ set plan
   - ○ idea

2. Mathematics is **required** if you are going to go to college.
   - ○ liked
   - ○ needed
   - ○ wished for
   - ○ good

3. Clyde's father tried to play the trombone but just got **disgusted** at his failure.
   - ○ excited about
   - ○ ashamed
   - ○ inspired
   - ○ mad and impatient

4. Sam was afraid to **annoy** Clyde by saying something he didn't like.
   - ○ bother
   - ○ cheer up
   - ○ tease
   - ○ sadden

Unit 3, Lesson 1

Part 2: Synonyms

Words that have nearly the same meaning are called **synonyms**. For example, **greedy** and **money-loving** both mean about the same thing. These two words are synonyms.

A. Darken the circle for the word from the list that is a synonym of the **boldfaced** word in the sentence.

1. The Hopi people have an old **custom** of throwing mud at weddings.
   - ○ wish
   - ○ joke
   - ○ practice
   - ○ idea

2. The mud that they throw is **sacred** so it very special and religious.
   - ○ thick
   - ○ holy
   - ○ yellow
   - ○ little

3. The father of the groom looked **wistful** as he remembered his own wedding.
   - ○ dreamy
   - ○ angry
   - ○ sad
   - ○ confused

4. Hopi weddings have much **hilarity** and fun.
   - ○ food
   - ○ silence
   - ○ pain
   - ○ laughter

5. Throwing the mud helps the two families deal with problems and **disputes** later.
   - ○ arguments
   - ○ children
   - ○ jokes
   - ○ meals

6. Mud throwers yell **insults** and bad things at each other.
   - ○ compliments
   - ○ sayings
   - ○ rude comments
   - ○ ideas

Unit 3, Lesson 1

Part 3: Compound Words

A **compound word** is a word made by putting two words together. Knowing the meaning of the smaller words helps you figure out the meaning of the whole word. For example, **fishbowl** is made of the smaller words *fish* and *bowl*. You can figure out that a fishbowl is a bowl in which fish live.

A. Combine each word in **Row 1** with a word in **Row 2** to make a compound word. Then write each compound word beside its definition below.

Row 1:   repair   straw   road   sun   under

Row 2:   berry   rise   man   growth   block

1. someone who fixes broken things   _____

2. something to stop traffic   _____

3. a sweet, red berry   _____

4. dawn   _____

5. plants that grow low to the ground   _____

B. Use a compound word from Exercise A to complete the following sentences. Then, see if you can find the other compound word in each sentence and circle it.

1. I love whipped cream on top of my _____ short cake.

2. The best time to catch fish is very early, at _____.

3. The police had formed a _____ to stop the robber.

4. Grandpa found an old turtle hiding in the _____ in the garden.

5. I called a _____ to fix the broken washing machine.

6. Sammy lost his Frisbee when it flew into the dense _____.

7. His hair was so red that it looked like a giant _____.

8. I had to get up at _____ when I delivered the morning paper.

9. It takes a smart _____ to fix a television.

10. The mudslide had crossed the highway and created a _____.

Power Words

Look at the words below. Circle any that you think you may know. Be ready to tell the class what the word means. Also tell the class how you think you know that word.

assassin	father-in-law	pillar	self-respect
course	imitate	pulse	short-lived
extinguished	mob	resigned	trade-in

Part 1: Context Clues

Remember that you can often figure out the meaning of an unknown word from the words that appear near by. The words or phrases that surround an unknown word are called **context clues**. For example, see how the second and third sentence below tells you that *dilipated* means old and broken down.

The old house was dilapidated. The steps, porch, and windows were broken.

A. Use context clues to figure out the meaning of the **bold** word. Darken in the circle with the correct definition.

1. The constant tapping of drums sounded like a steady **pulse**.
   - ○ hand
   - ○ beat
   - ○ music
   - ○ style

2. The sweet desserts are always my favorite **course** of a meal.
   - ○ appetizer
   - ○ part of a meal
   - ○ menu
   - ○ wish

3. The repairman was leaning against a **pillar** that held up the roof.
   - ○ column
   - ○ ramp
   - ○ building
   - ○ stairway

4. Finally the fire was **extinguished**, and the house was safe.
   - ○ controlled
   - ○ lit
   - ○ fed
   - ○ put out

Part 2: Synonyms

Words that have nearly the same meaning are called **synonyms**. For example, **small** and **tiny** both mean about the same thing. These two words are synonyms.

A. Read each of the following sentences. The words in the parentheses are synonyms. Think about which synonym best fits the meaning of the sentence. Underline the word in parentheses that best completes the sentence. Use a dictionary or the-saurus if necessary.

1. The robbers will (copy, steal, imitate) all the money they can.

2. My mom had to (bring, pull, inch) me to the dentist.

3. The pizza with the jalapenos and chili peppers tasted (sour, hot, pungent).

4. The (assassin, criminal, attacker) agreed to kill the president.

5. We went to the car (dash, contest, race) at the track in Daytona, Florida.

6. The motor on the boat (resigned, quit, left) when we got to the dock.

7. The angry (onlookers, throng, mob) yelled and threw stones.

8. David was always (last, terminal, closing) in every race he ran.

9. Would you please (dart, accelerate, hurry) because we are very late.

10. With all the new students, our class will (inflate, magnify, increase) this year.

11. I wanted to take a short (sleep, slumber, nap) before the dance.

12. When Sarah's dog died, she (wailed, cried, whimpered) all night.

13. The doughnuts were (full, flush, heaping) with strawberry jelly inside.

14. Juan had a small (portion, part, division) in the play.

15. My dad always picks the right (utensil, machine, tool) to fix the television.

Unit 3, Lesson 2

Part 3: Hyphenated Compound Words

You may remember that a **compound word** is two words joined together to form a new word with its own meaning. Sometimes a compound word is written with a hypen (-). For example, the compound word **home-style** has a hyphen.

A. Circle the compound words in these sentences. Then write the two words of each compound word on the lines below.

1. If you don't believe in yourself, you won't have any self-respect.

   _____ + _____

2. My dad loves to go fly-fishing in the streams of Idaho.

   _____ + _____

3. Sue's father-in-law was very nice at the wedding.

   _____ + _____ + _____

4. The old tape recorder was a reel-to-reel instead of a cassette.

   _____ + _____ + _____

5. In baseball, to bat in place of the regular scheduled batter is to pinch-hit.

   _____ + _____   _____ + _____

6. The life of a butterfly is very short-lived.

   _____ + _____   _____ + _____

7. The airplanes did a fly-over to make sure the enemy was retreating.

   _____ + _____   _____ + _____

8. My grandfather is very smart. His mind is like a steel-trap.

   _____ + _____   _____ + _____

9. Luis's father got a trade-in for the dishwasher and saved a lot of money.

   _____ + _____   _____ + _____

Power Words

Look at the words below. Circle any that you think you may know. Be ready to tell the class what the word means. Also tell the class how you think you know that word.

annoy	extinguished	pillar	sacred
assassin	father-in-law	pulse	self-respect
course	hilarity	repairman	short-lived
custom	imitate	required	system
disgusted	insults	resigned	trade-in
disputes	mob	roadblock	wistful

Part 1: Context Clues

Remember that you can figure out the meaning of an unknown word from the words that appear near by. These words or phrases are called **context clues**.

A. Use context clues to figure out the meaning of the **bold** word. Darken in the circle with the correct definition.

1. The coach was angry and **disgusted** with her team's play.
   - ○ glad
   - ○ sad
   - ○ excited
   - ○ mad and impatient

2. The library had four tall **pillars** that held up the front roof.
   - ○ signs
   - ○ columns
   - ○ people
   - ○ ramps

3. The music from the DJ had a steady **pulse** that was easy to dance to.
   - ○ beat
   - ○ band
   - ○ lyrics
   - ○ song

4. My little sister loves to hide my CDs just to **annoy** me. It makes me mad!
   - ○ sadden
   - ○ cheer up
   - ○ tease
   - ○ bother

Unit 3, Lesson 3

Part 2: Synonyms

Words that have nearly the same meaning are called **synonyms**. For example, **happy** and **glad** both mean about the same thing. These two words are synonyms.

A. Match the word in **Column A** with its synonym in **Column B**. Write the letter of the correct synonym in the blank provided. Use a dictionary or thesaurus if necessary.

Column A	Column B
1. _____ required	A. bother
2. _____ custom	B. laughter
3. _____ wistful	C. plan
4. _____ disputes	D. mad
5. _____ mob	E. beat
6. _____ insults	F. practice
7. _____ assassin	G. rudeness
8. _____ sacred	H. holy
9. _____ hilarity	I. column
10. _____ increase	J. dreamy
11. _____ annoy	K. magnify
12. _____ system	L. killer
13. _____ disgusted	M. crowd
14. _____ pillar	N. arguments
15. _____ pulse	O. needed

Unit 3, Lesson 3

Part 3: Compound Words

A **compound word** is a word made by putting two words together. Knowing the meaning of the smaller words helps you figure out the meaning of the whole word. For example, **fishbowl** is made of the smaller words *fish* and *bowl*. You can figure out that a fishbowl is a bowl in which fish live.

A. Draw a line between the two words in each compound word below. Then write the word's meaning on the line provided. Use a dictionary if necessary.

1. repairman: _____

2. roadblock: _____

3. undergrowth: _____

4. sunrise: _____

5. self-respect: _____

6. baseball: _____

7. dishwasher: _____

8. grandfather: _____

9. airplane: _____

10. trade-in: _____

B. Fluency: Practice reading the story below until you can read it smoothly. There are 14 of your **Power Words** in the story. Circle each one as you find it.

John, my father-in-law, was disgusted with the repairman when he came late. The man said he had a set system for driving through the city. His driving plan was short-lived, however, when he ran into a police roadblock. It seems the police were after a member of the mob who was an assassin.

John asked if it was the custom of criminals to annoy people trying to get to work. He said that disputes between the police and killers ought to be settled in another neighborhood. Criminals just don't have any self-respect.

Looking at the dishwasher, the man said that a lot would be required to fix it. It might be a better to get a trade-in. John saw no hilarity in this comment.

Part A: Context Clues

Directions: For each numbered blank, there is a list of words with the same number. Choose the word from each list that best completes the meaning of the paragraph.

1. Kim was _____. The last _____ of the meal was a serving of fried worms
   (1)   (2)
   and rotten eggs.

   1. ○ hungry   **2.** ○ course
           ○ neat   ○ fork
           ○ bored   ○ drink
           ○ disgusted   ○ cook

2. At dawn we stopped hearing the steady _____. Finally the loud drum music
                                          (3)
   was _____.
        (4)

   3. ○ dripping   **4.** ○ interesting
           ○ cry   ○ extinguished
           ○ pulse   ○ bad
           ○ chatter   ○ played

3. Sam could not change the old designer's or _____ set way of doing things. He
                                              (5)
   would have to build the column, or _____, in front of the door.
                                       (6)

   5. ○ system   **6.** ○ window
           ○ occupation   ○ roof
           ○ book   ○ pillar
           ○ reason   ○ desk

4. The teacher was beginning to _____ John. He couldn't quit though because this
                                (7)
   course was _____.
               (8)

   7. ○ worship   **8.** ○ history
           ○ annoy   ○ required
           ○ like   ○ old
           ○ see   ○ silly

Unit 3, Test

Part B: Synonyms

Directions: Fill in the letter of the word that is a synonym of the bold word.

1. angry **mob**
   - Ⓐ actor
   - Ⓑ crowd
   - Ⓒ dogs
   - Ⓓ bees
   - Ⓔ student

2. much **hilarity**
   - Ⓕ smell
   - Ⓖ wind
   - Ⓗ pain
   - Ⓘ music
   - Ⓙ fun

3. a terrible **assassin**
   - Ⓚ book
   - Ⓛ dream
   - Ⓜ killer
   - Ⓝ threat
   - Ⓞ fight

4. a **sacred** book
   - Ⓟ old
   - Ⓠ ancient
   - Ⓡ funny
   - Ⓢ holy
   - Ⓣ nasty

5. to **increase**
   - Ⓐ to test
   - Ⓑ to try out
   - Ⓒ to make smarter
   - Ⓓ to grow
   - Ⓔ to walk away

6. a useful **tool**
   - Ⓕ deal
   - Ⓖ job
   - Ⓗ loss
   - Ⓘ instrument
   - Ⓙ gamble

7. yell **insults**
   - Ⓚ ideas
   - Ⓛ reasons
   - Ⓜ bits of wisdom
   - Ⓝ rude comments
   - Ⓞ orders

8. a **wistful** look
   - Ⓟ dreamy
   - Ⓠ sorry
   - Ⓡ mad
   - Ⓢ bored
   - Ⓣ confused

9. an old **custom**
   - Ⓐ man
   - Ⓑ building
   - Ⓒ practice
   - Ⓓ boat
   - Ⓔ general

10. many **disputes**
    - Ⓕ parties
    - Ⓖ arguments
    - Ⓗ compliments
    - Ⓘ failures
    - Ⓙ sayings

Part C: Compound Words

Directions: Match the meaning of the compound word in **Column B** with the word in **Column A**. Fill in the letter of the definition on the blank provided.

Column A

1. _____ father-in-law
2. _____ roadblock
3. _____ self-respect
4. _____ airplane
5. _____ strawberry
6. _____ repairman
7. _____ butterfly
8. _____ pinch-hit
9. _____ sunrise
10. _____ undergrowth
11. _____ short-lived
12. _____ reel-to-reel
13. _____ dishwasher
14. _____ trade-in
15. _____ grandfather

Column B

A. dawn

B. to take pride in oneself

C. the father of a mother or father

D. to bat at baseball when it is not one's turn

E. a device to wash dishes automatically

F. an insect with broad, colorful wings

G. a car or appliance that is used

H. plants that grow under taller plants or trees

I. a blockage in a path or roadway

J. a recording device with tape on two reels

K. one who repairs or fixes something

L. a self-powered machine that flies in the air

M. a short life span

N. a berry with a red color and sweet taste

O. the father of a husband or wife

Directions: Each of the following compound words has been divided into its base words in two ways. Only one choice is correct. Write the letter of the correct choice in the blank provided.

1. _____ repairman   A. re / pairman   B. repair / man
2. _____ undergrowth   A. und / ergrowth   B. under / growth
3. _____ butterfly   A. but / terfly   B. butter / fly
4. _____ grandfather   A. grand / father   B. gran / dfather

Power Words

Look at the words below. Circle any that you think you may know. Be ready to tell the class what the word means. Also tell the class how you think you know that word.

affliction	cooperate	imposter	postgraduate
banished	defog	merciful	route
bearing	heir	pause	semicircle

Part 1: Prefixes and Base Words

A **base word** is a word that can stand alone. A **prefix** is a word part added to the beginning of a base word. For example, in the word **defrost**, *frost* is the base word and **de-** is the prefix added at the beginning. Knowing the meaning of a prefix helps you figure out the meaning of the whole word. *Defrost* means "unfreeze." Study the meaning of the following prefixes until you can remember what each means.

de- means "make the opposite of" / **post-** means "after"
co- means "together, equally, jointly" / **semi-** means "half"

A. Draw a line between the base word and the prefix for each word below. Then write what the word means on the line. Use a dictionary if necessary.

1. postgraduate - _____

2. semipro - _____

3. coworker - _____

4. defog - _____

5. postoperative - _____

6. cooperate - _____

7. semisoft - _____

8. coexist - _____

9. derail - _____

10. semicircle - _____

11. cosign - _____

12. semiannual - _____

Unit 4, Lesson 1

Part 2: Context Clues

Remember that you can often figure out the meaning of an unknown word from the words that appear nearby. The words or phrases that surround an unknown word are called **context clues**. For example, see how the words in the sentences below tells you that *depressed* means very sad.

Jean was *depressed* over losing her dog. She cried all night long.

A. Use context clues to figure out the meaning of the **boldfaced** word. Darken in the circle with the correct definition.

1. Tom, who was terrified of being killed, asked the king to be **merciful**.
   - ○ generous
   - ○ kind
   - ○ quick
   - ○ royal

2. The king was worried that his son, the **heir** to the throne, had gone mad.
   - ○ the person who gets another's money and title
   - ○ the person who becomes the queen
   - ○ the person who rebuilds the throne itself
   - ○ the person who gives up his money at birth

3. Tom was unable to convince the king that he was not his son; he was an **impostor**.
   - ○ enemy
   - ○ artist
   - ○ someone pretending to be someone else
   - ○ someone trying to kill the king

4. One father had **banished** his son by sending him to prison.
   - ○ sent away
   - ○ beaten
   - ○ turned on
   - ○ cared for

5. The prince had a very noble **bearing**, carrying himself well.
   - ○ dress
   - ○ home
   - ○ behavior
   - ○ son

6. The prince did not know that the king's **affliction** would eventually kill him.
   - ○ dog
   - ○ wife
   - ○ attitude
   - ○ sickness

Unit 4, Lesson 1

Part 3: Homophones

Words that sound the same but have different spellings and meanings are called **homophones**. For example, **meat** and **meet** are homophones. Here are some other examples of homophones.

here and **hear**	**steak** and **stake**	**paws** and **pause**
root and **route**	**see** and **sea**	**tide** and **tied**
plane and **plain**	**its** and **it's**	**tow** and **toe**

A. Decide which of the homophones above answer the questions. Write the correct homophone in the blank. Use a dictionary if necessary.

1. What comes from a cow?   _____

2. What do you follow when you're driving?   _____

3. What do you use your ears for?   _____

4. What is high and low about the ocean?   _____

5. What do you use your eyes for?   _____

6. What flies you around the country?   _____

7. If it's not there, it must be where?   _____

8. What holds a plant to the ground?   _____

9. What do you call a cat's feet?   _____

10. What must you do to a broken down car?   _____

B. Circle the two homophones in each sentence. Write a brief definition of each. Use a dictionary if necessary.

1. That cow who is tied to the stake will soon become a steak.

   _____

2. It's always funny to watch a dog chase its tail.

   _____

3. The plane had to make a crash landing on the plain.

   _____

Power Words

Look at the words below. Circle any that you think you may know. Be ready to tell the class what the word means. Also tell the class how you think you know that word.

adaptable	constantly	occupy	regretfully
bravely	lengthwise	quarry	spotless
cheerful	nomad	recollect	truthful

Part 1: Suffixes and Base Words

A **base word** is a word that can stand alone. A **suffix** is a word part added to the beginning of a base word. For example, in the word **homeless,** *home* is the base word and *-less* is the suffix added at the end. Knowing the meaning of a suffix helps you figure out the meaning of the whole word. *Homeless* means "without a home." Study the meaning of the following suffixes until you can remember what each means.

-ful means "full of" / *-less* means "without"
-wise means "in a specified way" / *-ly* tells how something is done

A. Read each sentence. Use your knowledge of suffixes and base words to help you figure out the meaning of the underlined word. Write its meaning on the line provided. Use a dictionary if necessary.

1. Serena measured the box <u>lengthwise</u> to make sure it would fit.

   lengthwise means: _____

2. My car was <u>spotless</u> when it came out of the new car wash downtown.

   spotless means:_____

3. You are a lot more <u>cheerful</u> since you made the soccer team.

   cheerful means:_____

4. The troops <u>bravely</u> entered the battle.

   bravely means: _____

5. One of Marco's greatest qualities is that he is always <u>truthful</u>.

   truthful means: _____

6. Shelley is <u>constantly</u> spending money.

   constantly means:_____

Unit 4, Lesson 2

Part 2: Context Clues

Remember that you can often figure out the meaning of an unknown word from the words that appear near by. The words or phrases that surround an unknown word are called **context clues**.

A. Use context clues to figure out the meaning of the **bold** word. Darken in the circle with the correct definition.

1. Our family was more than ready to **occupy** the new house. We wanted to move.
   ○ clean
   ○ paint
   ○ stay in
   ○ finish

2. My dad told us **regretfully** that we couldn't go on vacation.
   ○ sadly
   ○ happily
   ○ quietly
   ○ rapidly

3. Tom couldn't **recollect** when he last ate a jelly doughnut.
   ○ come
   ○ wish
   ○ taste
   ○ remember

4. The **nomad** traveled from place to place without settling down.
   ○ man
   ○ wanderer
   ○ housewife
   ○ infant

5. The men went to the **quarry** to dig for marble and slate.
   ○ store
   ○ place to mine stone
   ○ farm
   ○ building

6. My mother is very **adaptable**. Nothing seems to bother her.
   ○ eager
   ○ silly
   ○ flexible
   ○ funny

Unit 4, Lesson 2

Part 3: Homophones

Remember that words that sound the same but have different spellings and meanings are called **homophones**. For example, **to, two,** and **too** are homophones.

A. Circle the homophones in each sentence. Then write a brief definition of each homophone on the line provided. Use a dictionary if necessary.

1. Our family walked in the door at the local inn.

   _____

2. Sean was in a daze for days after hitting his head.

   _____

3. I wouldn't want to be the one stung by a bee.

   _____

4. We had to flee the pet store because Marty was bitten by a flea.

   _____

5. It was just like him to hum a hymn at the dinner table.

   _____

6. We found a piece of fur stuck to the fir tree on our camping trip.

   _____

7. You will find that getting fined by the police is no fun.

   _____

8. When Kim prays, she gives praise to all the people who have helped her.

   _____

9. We were very tense sitting inside our tents when we heard the bear growl.

   _____

10. Sam had to peer down the fishing pier to find his younger brother.

   _____

Power Words Review

Look at the words below. Circle any that you think you may know. Be ready to tell the class what the word means. Also tell the class how you think you know that word.

adaptable	constantly	merciful	recollect
affliction	cooperate	nomad	regretfully
banished	defog	occupy	route
bearing	heir	pause	semicircle
bravely	imposter	postgraduate	spotless
cheerful	lengthwise	quarry	truthful

Part 1: Affixes and Base Words

Remember that a **base word** is a word that can stand alone. An **affix** is a word part added to the beginning or end of a base word. **Prefixes** and **suffixes** are affixes. Knowing the meaning of an affix helps you figure out the meaning of the whole word. Study the meaning of the following affixes until you can remember what each means.

de- means "make the opposite of" / *post-* means "after"
co- means "together, equally, jointly" / *semi-* means "half"
-ful means "full of" / *-less* means "without"
-wise means "in a specified way" / *-ly* tells how something is done

A. Match the word in **Column A** with its meaning in **Column B**. Remember to break the word parts into their prefixes, suffixes, and base words. Use a dictionary if needed.

Column A

1. _____ defog
2. _____ lengthwise
3. _____ cheerful
4. _____ semicircle
5. _____ cooperate
6. _____ constantly
7. _____ spotless
8. _____ postgraduate
9. _____ bravely
10. _____ merciful

Column B

A. very clean
B. with great courage
C. to work together
D. full of happiness or cheer
E. very kind
F. to remove vapor or fog
G. to measure the length of something
H. a half of a circle
I. repeatedly, without stopping
J. after graduation

Unit 4, Lesson 3

Part 2: Context Clues

Remember that you can often figure out the meaning of an unknown word from the words that appear nearby. The words or phrases that surround an unknown word are called **context clues**.

A. Use context clues to figure out the meaning of the **boldfaced** word. Darken in the circle with the correct definition.

1. The evil prince was **banished** and told to never return to his land.
   - ○ hated
   - ○ kind
   - ○ sent away
   - ○ royal

2. Bonnie is so **adaptable**. She changes with the times and situations.
   - ○ young
   - ○ flexible
   - ○ different
   - ○ odd

3. Our principal has a **bearing** of power and respectfulness.
   - ○ title
   - ○ job
   - ○ vision
   - ○ composure

4. My sister couldn't **recollect** where she put her car keys.
   - ○ remember
   - ○ share
   - ○ care
   - ○ see

5. My aunt has such a bad **affliction** that she went to see a doctor.
   - ○ cousin
   - ○ sickness
   - ○ behavior
   - ○ dream

6. Sally told me she would **occupy** my seat and I could leave.
   - ○ stay in
   - ○ sell
   - ○ trade
   - ○ buy

Part 3: Homophones

Words that sound the same but have different spellings and meanings are called **homophones**. For example, **pour** and **poor** are homophones.

A. In the blank provided, write a homophone for each of the words below. Use a dictionary if necessary.

1. days _____

2. find _____

3. peer _____

4. steak _____

5. see _____

6. in _____

7. tense _____

8. tied _____

9. route _____

10. toe _____

11. fur _____

12. flee _____

B. Fluency: Practice reading the story below until you can read it smoothly. There are sixteen homophones in the story; however, each of them is the wrong word. Circle the incorrect homophone and write the correct word above it.

A man once decided to flea his land. He took a plain across the see. Halfway in his root, he began to here a bad noise. He crashed inn the ocean and floated on the tied for three daze. He became very tents and began to sing a him to feel better. A week later a young man was sitting on a peer and saw something in the water. What could it bee? He called the Coast Guard to toe the man in. The man was very grateful. He didn't think anyone would fined him." Its a miracle," he said. "Now, where can I get a good stake?"

Part A: Affixes and Base Words

Directions: Match the word in **Column A** with its definition in **Column B**. Write the letter of the correct definition in the blank provided.

Column A

1. _____ coworker
2. _____ lengthwise
3. _____ semicircle
4. _____ constantly
5. _____ cooperate
6. _____ defrost
7. _____ cheerful
8. _____ semiannual
9. _____ bravely
10. _____ postgraduate
11. _____ coexist
12. _____ spotless
13. _____ truthful
14. _____ semisoft
15. _____ homeless

Column B

A. courageously

B. after graduation

C. to unfreeze

D. work together

E. partly soft

F. to live together

G. very clean

H. honest

I. along the length of something

J. repeatedly

K. without a home

L. twice a year

M. colleague; someone you work with

N. happy

O. half circle

Directions: The following words have been divided both correctly and incorrectly into their affixes and base words. Write the letter of the correctly divided word on the blank.

1. _____   A. coex / ist   B. co / exist
2. _____   A. semi / soft   B. sem / isoft
3. _____   A. tru / thful   B. truth / ful
4. _____   A. brav / ely   B. brave / ly

Unit 4, Test

Part B: Context Clues

Directions: For each numbered blank, there is a list of words with the same number. Choose the word from each list that best completes the meaning of the paragraph.

1. Ahmed was a _____. The king had _____ him from the country so he was
   forced to wander from place to place.
   _____(1)_____   _____(2)_____

1.	salesman	**2.**	paused
	nomad		banished
	postgraduate		raided
	champion		wed

2. Margaret had a bad _____. Now that she was sick, she was unable to
   _____(3)_____
   _____ anything that happened in the past.
   ___(4)___

3.	neighbor	**4.**	recollect
	recollect		cooperate
	affliction		buy
	sister		wish for

3. Edward was a(n) _____. Everyone knew he was not the real _____ to the
   _____(5)_____   _____(6)_____
   throne after the king died.

5.	athlete	**6.**	prince
	nomad		quarry
	executive		heir
	impostor		buyer

4. My mother is very _____. She must _____ a house where there are seven
   _____(7)_____   _____(8)_____
   children who need her to do many different things.

7.	bravely	**8.**	occupy
	weird		spotless
	adaptable		wash
	old		buy

Name _____ Date _____

Part C: Homophones

Directions: Fill in the letter of the word that is a homophone of the **bold** word.

1. days
   - Ⓐ dade
   - Ⓑ dail
   - Ⓒ date
   - Ⓓ daze
   - Ⓔ dead

2. peer
   - Ⓕ pear
   - Ⓖ pierce
   - Ⓗ pert
   - Ⓘ peel
   - Ⓙ pier

3. tide
   - Ⓚ tid
   - Ⓛ tite
   - Ⓜ tied
   - Ⓝ tye
   - Ⓞ tie

4. root
   - Ⓟ rut
   - Ⓠ route
   - Ⓡ roote
   - Ⓢ rute
   - Ⓣ rude

5. him
   - Ⓐ hen
   - Ⓑ hymn
   - Ⓒ hin
   - Ⓓ whim
   - Ⓔ when

6. tow
   - Ⓕ to
   - Ⓖ toad
   - Ⓗ oh
   - Ⓘ too
   - Ⓙ toe

7. flea
   - Ⓚ fly
   - Ⓛ fli
   - Ⓜ flee
   - Ⓝ fee
   - Ⓞ free

8. paws
   - Ⓟ pause
   - Ⓠ pass
   - Ⓡ past
   - Ⓢ posse
   - Ⓣ post

9. tents
   - Ⓐ ten
   - Ⓑ tin
   - Ⓒ tend
   - Ⓓ tense
   - Ⓔ tint

10. steak
   - Ⓕ stick
   - Ⓖ stack
   - Ⓗ stake
   - Ⓘ stay
   - Ⓙ steck

Power Words

Look at the words below. Circle any that you think you may know. Be ready to tell the class what the word means. Also tell the class how you think you know that word.

cast	documentary	mentor	reversal
casually	memoir	monopolize	revert
consumed	memorial	refined	sensible

Part 1: Antonyms

Words that have nearly <u>opposite</u> meanings are called **antonyms**. For example, **beautiful** and **ugly** mean the opposite of each other. These two words are antonyms.

A. Darken the circle for the word from the list that is an antonym of the **boldfaced** word in the sentence. Use the ideas in the sentence to help you make your choice.

1. Not caring how clean the house was, David **casually** swept the room.
   - ○ eventually
   - ○ seriously
   - ○ slowly
   - ○ helplessly

2. When everyone gets off work, the trains and roads are very **crowded**.
   - ○ filled
   - ○ loud
   - ○ empty
   - ○ hot

3. Ms. James will always greet you with a **smile**.
   - ○ candy
   - ○ handshake
   - ○ kiss
   - ○ frown

4. The mist was **rising** out of the ground like a spooky fog.
   - ○ falling
   - ○ sneaking
   - ○ creeping
   - ○ climbing

5. Ahmed is such a **kind** person, always helping other people.
   - ○ dull
   - ○ mean
   - ○ old
   - ○ young

Unit 5, Lesson 1

Part 2: Latin Roots

Many English words are made up of word parts from other languages, especially Greek and Latin. These word parts are called **roots**. A root cannot stand alone, but knowing its meaning helps you figure out the meaning of the whole word. A group of words with the same root is called a **word family**. Study the chart of **Latin** roots below.

Root	Meaning	Example
doc	teach	document
sens/sent	feel	sensitive
vert/ver	turn	reverse
mem/ment	mind	mental
not	note, mark	note

A. Underline the root of each word in **Column A**. Then match each word with its correct meaning in **Column B**. Write the letter of the correct meaning in the space provided. Use a dictionary if necessary.

Column A

1. _____ sensible

2. _____ doctrine

3. _____ revert

4. _____ mentor

5. _____ notation

6. _____ documentary

7. _____ memoir

8. _____ reversal

9. _____ memorial

10. _____ sensation

Column B

A. to turn completely around

B. an account of a person's experiences

C. a brief note

D. a statement of law or government

E. a physical or emotional feeling

F. something to celebrate the memory of a person or event

G. a teacher or guide

H. a work, such as a film, that presents facts

J. to turn back to the way things were

K. acting with or exhibiting good sense or judgment

Part 3: Shades of Meaning

Words may have small differences in meaning. A reader must know the exact meaning of a word to understand what the writer is saying. For example, a boat that is *large* is different from a boat that is *huge*. Huge is much bigger than large.

A. Read the sentence with the missing word. Then read the question about the missing word. Choose the word that best answers the question.

1. All of Marty's ideas were _____ by the end of the meeting.

   Which of these words would indicate that all of Marty's ideas were used up?

   A. spoken
   B. silenced
   C. consumed
   D. left

2. Jose can _____ his fishing line over sixty feet into the river.

   Which of these words would indicate Jose just can throw his line far?

   A. cast
   B. lay
   C. hook
   D. reel

3. Paul likes to _____ the conversation at every party.

   Which of these words would indicate that Paul controls all the conversation?

   A. reply to
   B. listen to
   C. question
   D. monopolize

4. The sugar is _____ at the factory before it is shipped to the stores.

   Which of these words would indicate that the sugar is made pure?

   A. poured
   B. refined
   C. bagged
   D. heated

Power Words

Look at the words below. Circle any that you think you may know. Be ready to tell the class what the word means. Also tell the class how you think you know that word.

accessible	deport	malfunction	pursue
data	equitable	predicament	transport
defunct	equivalent	propel	vocation

Part 1: Antonyms

Words that have nearly <u>opposite</u> meanings are called **antonyms**. For example, **fat** and **thin** mean the opposite of each other. These two words are antonyms.

A. Darken the circle for the word from the list that is an antonym of the **boldfaced** word in the sentence. Use the ideas in the sentence to help you make your choice.

1. Jessica **rued** the day that she had gotten her speeding ticket.
   - ○ hated
   - ○ loved
   - ○ wished for
   - ○ remembered

2. Everyone felt **safe** with the policemen standing nearby.
   - ○ danger
   - ○ peace
   - ○ bored
   - ○ hot

3. Orange juice is a **natural** substance.
   - ○ filtered
   - ○ tasty
   - ○ bad
   - ○ artificial

4. Every chocolate in the box was **sweet**.
   - ○ nasty
   - ○ sour
   - ○ sugary
   - ○ flavorful

5. We were glad when the elevator was **moving**.
   - ○ going
   - ○ replaced
   - ○ rebuilt
   - ○ still

Unit 5, Lesson 2

Part 2: Latin Roots

Many English words are made up of word parts from other languages, especially Greek and Latin. These word parts are called **roots**. A root cannot stand alone, but knowing its meaning helps you figure out the meaning of the whole word. A group of words with the same root is called a **word family**. Study the chart of **Latin** roots below.

Root	Meaning	Example
funct	perform	function
pel/puls	drive, thrust, urge, throb	propeller
voc	voice, call	vocal
equi	equal	equidistant
port	carry	airport

A. Underline the root of each word in **Column A**. Then match each word with its correct meaning in **Column B**. Write the letter of the correct meaning in the space provided. Use a dictionary if necessary.

Column A

1. _____ equitable

2. _____ transport

3. _____ vocation

4. _____ propel

5. _____ pulse

6. _____ malfunction

7. _____ equivalent

8. _____ vocabulary

9. _____ deport

10. _____ defunct

Column B

A. to push forward

B. to force one to leave a place

C. no longer working or functional

D. to carry from one place to another

E. a steady surge or beat

F. to break or to stop working

G. fair and equal

H. one's job or calling

J. all the words of a language

K. having equal value

Unit 5, Lesson 2

Part 3: Shades of Meaning

Words may have small differences in meaning. A reader must know the exact meaning of a word to understand what the writer is saying. For example, a boat that is *nearby* is different from a boat that is *here*. Here is much closer than nearby.

A. Read the sentence with the missing word. Then read the question about the missing word. Choose the word that best answers the question.

1. The quarterback was _____ by the other team as he ran for the touchdown.

    Which of these words would indicate that the quarterback was chased?

    A. tackled
    B. run
    C. pursued
    D. led

2. The teacher gave us lots of _____ to help us make a decision.

    Which of these words would indicate that the teacher gave lots of information?

    A. time
    B. data
    C. work
    D. exercises

3. The hiker who had fallen into the river was in quite a _____.

    Which of these words would indicate that hiker was in a difficult situation?

    A. trick
    B. party
    C. discovery
    D. predicament

4. The office is on the first floor and very _____.

    Which of these words would indicate that the office is easy to reach?

    A. big
    B. accessible
    C. comfortable
    D. sanitary

Power Words Review

Look at the words below. Circle any that you think you may know. Be ready to tell the class what the word means. Try to use the word in a sentence to show its meaning.

accessible	deport	memorial	refined
cast	documentary	mentor	reversal
casually	equitable	monopolize	revert
consumed	equivalent	predicament	sensible
data	malfunction	propel	transport
defunct	memoir	pursue	vocation

Part 1: Antonyms

Remember that words that have nearly opposite meanings are called **antonyms**.

A. Match the word in **Column A** with its antonym in **Column B**. Write the letter of the correct antonym in the blank provided.

Column A

1. _____ crowded

2. _____ rued

3. _____ natural

4. _____ smile

5. _____ rising

6. _____ moving

7. _____ safe

8. _____ kind

9. _____ sweet

10. _____ casually

Column B

A. mean

B. danger

C. sour

D. empty

E. artificial

F. still

G. seriously

H. loved

I. frown

J. falling

Name _____   Date _____

Part 2: Latin Roots

Many English words are made up of word parts from other languages, especially Greek and Latin. These word parts are called **roots**. Study the chart of **Latin** roots below.

Root	Meaning	Example
doc	teach	<u>doc</u>ument
sens/sent	feel	<u>sens</u>itive
vert/ver	turn	re<u>ver</u>se
mem/ment	mind	<u>ment</u>al
not	note, mark	<u>not</u>e
funct	perform	<u>funct</u>ion
pel/puls	drive, thrust, urge, throb	pro<u>pel</u>ler
voc	voice, call	<u>voc</u>al
equi	equal	<u>equi</u>distant
port	carry	air<u>port</u>

A. Match each word in **Column A** with its correct meaning in **Column B**. Write the letter of the correct meaning in the space provided. Use a dictionary if necessary.

Column A

1. _____ sensible

2. _____ documentary

3. _____ revert

4. _____ vocation

5. _____ malfunction

6. _____ equivalent

7. _____ memoir

8. _____ transport

Column B

A. to turn back to the way things were

B. an account of a person's experiences

C. to break or function improperly

D. having equal value

E. acting with good sense or judgment

F. to carry from one place to another

G. a work, such as a film, that presents facts

H. one's job or calling

Part 3: Shades of Meaning

Remember that words may have small differences in meaning. A reader must know the exact meaning of a word to understand what the writer is saying.

A. Read the sentence with the missing word. Then read the question about the missing word. Choose the word that best answers the question.

1. My sister loves to _____ the conversation at every party.

   Which of these words would indicate that the sister controls the conversation?

   A. listen to
   B. reply to
   C. monopolize
   D. question

2. Our class gathers lots of _____ by interviewing our classmates.

   Which of these words would indicate the class gathered information?

   A. data
   B. points
   C. money
   D. work

3. The sugar is _____ and then packaged in cardboard containers.

   Which of these words would indicate that the sugar is made pure?

   A. squeezed
   B. poured
   C. refined
   D. boiled

4. When Steve fell out of the boat he was in quite a _____.

   Which of these words would indicate that Steve was in a difficult situation?

   A. lake
   B. trip
   C. place
   D. predicament

Part A: Antonyms

Directions: Fill in the letter of the word that is an antonym of the **boldfaced** word.

1. **sweet**
   Ⓐ nice
   Ⓑ friendly
   Ⓒ sour
   Ⓓ wise
   Ⓔ sugary

2. **kind**
   Ⓕ mean
   Ⓖ nice
   Ⓗ trusting
   Ⓘ lovable
   Ⓙ wise

3. **moving**
   Ⓚ watching
   Ⓛ sailing
   Ⓜ active
   Ⓝ staring
   Ⓞ still

4. **casually**
   Ⓟ quietly
   Ⓠ seriously
   Ⓡ hardly
   Ⓢ daily
   Ⓣ lovely

5. **natural**
   Ⓐ filtered
   Ⓑ old
   Ⓒ tasty
   Ⓓ artificial
   Ⓔ bad

6. **rued**
   Ⓕ hated
   Ⓖ wished
   Ⓗ dreamed
   Ⓘ loved
   Ⓙ wanted

7. **smile**
   Ⓚ snore
   Ⓛ grin
   Ⓜ frown
   Ⓝ stare
   Ⓞ nod

8. **safe**
   Ⓟ danger
   Ⓠ lovely
   Ⓡ peaceful
   Ⓢ hot
   Ⓣ bored

9. **rising**
   Ⓐ falling
   Ⓑ feeling
   Ⓒ making
   Ⓓ wailing
   Ⓔ wrecking

10. **crowded**
    Ⓕ full
    Ⓖ large
    Ⓗ obese
    Ⓘ empty
    Ⓙ loud

Unit 5, Test

Part B: Latin Roots

Directions: Match the meaning of the word in **Column B** with the word in **Column A**. Fill in the letter of the definition on the blank provided.

Column A

1. _____ memoir
2. _____ equivalent
3. _____ vocation
4. _____ sensible
5. _____ documentary
6. _____ revert
7. _____ transport
8. _____ malfunction
9. _____ reversal
10. _____ memorial
11. _____ propel
12. _____ deport
13. _____ defunct
14. _____ mentor
15. _____ notation

Column B

A. a brief note

B. acting with good sense or judgment

C. to break or stop working

D. to push forward

E. to turn completely around

F. a teacher or guide

G. to force someone to leave a place

H. something to celebrate a person or event

I. no longer working or functional, useless

J. having equal value

K. to carry from one place to another

L. one's job or calling

M. an account of a person's life

N. a work, such as a film, that presents facts

O. to go back to the way things were

Directions: Each Latin and Greek root below has two definitions. Only one is correct. Write the letter of the correct one on the blank provided.

1. _____ mem, ment   A.   mind   B.   note

2. _____ funct   A.   perform   B.   turn

3. _____ vert, ver   A.   drive   B.   turn

4. _____ sens, sent   A.   feel   B.   voice

Unit 5, Test

Part C: Shades of Meaning

Directions: Read the sentence with the missing word. Then read the question about the missing word. Choose the word that best answers the question.

1. The campers _____ all the snacks and had nothing to eat after dark.

   Which of these words would indicate that the campers used up the snacks?

   A. tasted
   B. packed
   C. tried
   D. consumed

2. The library with the new ramps is _____ to all students.

   Which of these words would indicate that the library is easy to reach?

   A. affordable
   B. accessible
   C. necessary
   D. useful

3. Stuart's dad _____ the conversation in the car.

   Which of these words would indicate that Stuart's dad controls the conversation?

   A. questions
   B. makes
   C. monopolizes
   D. listens to

4. The computer produced more _____ than we could use.

   Which of these words would indicate that the computer produced a lot of information?

   A. data
   B. paper
   C. stuff
   D. noise

Power Words

Look at the words below. Circle any that you think you may know. Be ready to tell the class what the word means. Also tell the class how you think you know that word.

contraband	idiotic	midsummer	overspend
counteract	imbecile	midtown	ruler
deluded	junk	oversee	sinister

Part 1: Context Clues

Remember that you can often figure out the meaning of an unknown word from the words that appear nearby. The words or phrases that surround an unknown word are called **context clues**. For example, see how the words in the sentences below tell you that *depressed* means very sad.

> Jean was depressed over losing her dog. She cried all night long.

A. Use context clues to figure out the meaning of the **boldfaced** word. Darken in the circle with the correct definition.

1. Stars falling at night were a **sinister** sign that bad things would happen.
   - ○ good
   - ○ frequent
   - ○ evil
   - ○ old

2. The villagers thought Han was an **imbecile** for the stupid things he did as a child.
   - ○ genius
   - ○ problem
   - ○ idiot
   - ○ odd one

3. Most people believed that building a bridge for ants was an **idiotic** thing to do.
   - ○ stupid
   - ○ heavenly
   - ○ wise
   - ○ humorous

4. Han **deluded** the angry soldiers into thinking he was a stupid person.
   - ○ prayed
   - ○ wished
   - ○ fooled
   - ○ told

Unit 6, Lesson 1

Part 2: Multiple-Meaning Words

The word *multiple* means many. **Multiple-meaning words** are words that have more than one meaning. For example, the word *fly* can mean to sail through the air. It can also be a type of insect.

A. Read each sentence below. Think about how the **boldfaced** word in the sentence is used. Then read the different meanings of that word below. Write the letter of the definition in the blank that matches the meaning of the bold word in the sentence.

_____1. Han was thought to be a **ward** of the great god Shen.
   a. a part of a city or town
   b. a child under protection

_____2. A bright **star** in the night told the villagers that Han's birthday was special.
   a. a celebrity or famous person
   b. a heavenly body made up of burning gases

_____3. Han remained out in the **open** when it began to rain.
   a. to unwrap or uncover
   b. a space having no boundaries or walls
   c. a store that is ready to do business

_____4. The ants would remember Han's help and do him a **service** someday in return.
   a. a branch of the armed forces, for example, the navy or army
   b. a religious ceremony
   c. a favor, often in return for something

_____5. The prince's spear was as long as the mast on a sea-going **junk**.
   a. a Chinese ship with sails
   b. something thrown away or discarded

_____6. Han went to the **ruler** and offered him his services.
   a. a stick used to measure things
   b. the person in charge of a land, such as a king

_____7. The prince did not think Han was big and strong enough to **serve** in his army.
   a. to put a ball in play, as in the sport of tennis
   b. to fight or undergo military service
   c. to prepare and offer food

_____8. Han longed to turn his **steps** homeward.
   a. a manner of walking
   b. stairs

Unit 6, Lesson 1

Part 3: Prefixes and Base Words

A **base word** is a word that can stand alone. A **prefix** is a word part added to the beginning of a base word. For example, in the word **midyear,** *year* is the base word and *mid-* is the prefix added at the beginning. Knowing the meaning of a prefix helps you figure out the meaning of the whole word. *Midyear* means "halfway through the year." Study the meaning of the following prefixes until you can remember what each means.

> *counter-* means "opposite" or "contrary" / *over-* means "above" or "superior"
> *circum-* means "around" / *contra-* means "opposed" or "against"
> *mid-* means "halfway"

A. Draw a line between the base word and the prefix for each word below. Then write what the word means on the line. Use a dictionary if necessary.

1. counterargument - _____

2. oversee -_____

3. contraband - _____

4. midday - _____

5. circumnavigate -_____

6. overspend - _____

7. counterclaim -_____

8. circumference - _____

9. midsummer - _____

10. contradict - _____

11. counteract - _____

12. midtown - _____

Power Words

Look at the words below. Circle any that you think you may know. Be ready to tell the class what the word means. Also tell the class how you think you know that word.

comrade	musician	seaworthy	trustworthy
disintegrated	operator	skyward	uninhabited
lengthen	quicken	terrain	warlike

Part 1: Context Clues

Remember that you can often figure out the meaning of an unknown word from the words that appear nearby. The words or phrases that surround an unknown word are called **context clues**. For example, see how the words in the sentences below tell you that *composed* means to stay calm and not be bothered by things.

> Juan was always composed. Nothing ever seemed to bother him.

A. Use context clues to figure out the meaning of the **boldfaced** word. Darken in the circle with the correct definition.

1. The pilot's airplane **disintegrated** when it was blasted by the enemy rocket.
   - ○ dodged
   - ○ landed
   - ○ broke apart
   - ○ escaped

2. As he landed in the dense jungle, he knew he was in rough **terrain.**
   - ○ gear
   - ○ uniform
   - ○ luck
   - ○ countryside

3. The nearest village looked **uninhabited** because he could see no one.
   - ○ without water
   - ○ without people
   - ○ without houses
   - ○ scary

4. The pilot gave up on ever seeing again his **comrades** with whom he had flown.
   - ○ planes
   - ○ enemies
   - ○ friends
   - ○ children

Unit 6, Lesson 2

Part 2: Multiple-Meaning Words

The word *multiple* means many. **Multiple-meaning words** are words that have more than one meaning. For example, the word *craft* can mean a skill someone has. It can also be a type of boat.

A. Read each sentence below. Think about how the **boldfaced** word in the sentence is used. Then read the different meanings of that word below. Write the letter of the definition in the blank that matches the meaning of the boldfaced word in the sentence.

_____1. The pilot was the weapons **operator** on the airplane.
   a. a person who gets what they want through illegal or mean ways
   b. a person who operates a machine

_____2. When the pilot ejected, he saw the plane **blast** apart.
   a. a strong wind
   b. an explosion

_____3. The pilot smashed down through the leafy **branches**.
   a. the stems of a tree or bush
   b. a part of a larger system, such as a branch of a river

_____4. Hiding in the jungle **growth** for weeks, the pilot became very tired and weak.
   a. the process of growing
   b. something that grows, such as plants

_____5. When he heard the enemy nearby, he **froze** in his tracks.
   a. stopped
   b. became frozen due to very low temperature

_____6. It was impossible to **cross** the river without being seen and captured.
   a. an upright post with a piece at a right angle
   b. to be angry
   c. to pass from one side to another

_____7. The pilot pushed the radio **button** and called for help.
   a. a round object used to fasten parts of clothing together
   b. the tip of a rattlesnake's rattle
   c. a switch that is pushed

_____8. Finally the **chopper** lifted the pilot out of the jungle and flew him to safety.
   a. motorcycle
   b. helicopter
   c. a person that chops things apart

Part 3: Suffixes and Base Words

A **base word** is a word that can stand alone. A **suffix** is a word part added to the end of a base word. For example, in the word **ghostlike,** *ghost* is the base word and *-like* is the suffix added at the end. Knowing the meaning of a suffix helps you figure out the meaning of the whole word. *Ghostlike* means "looking like a ghost." Study the meaning of the following suffixes until you can remember what each means.

-ward means "toward" / *-en* means "to become"
-like mean "similar to" or "like" / *-worthy* means "safe for" or "suitable"
-ician means "person who does something"

A. Draw a line between the base word and the suffix for each word below. Then write what the word means on the line. Use a dictionary if necessary.

1. upward - _____

2. strengthen - _____

3. seaworthy - _____

4. ladylike - _____

5. skyward - _____

6. beautician - _____

7. lengthen - _____

8. trustworthy - _____

9. warlike - _____

10. musician - _____

11. quicken - _____

12. homeward - _____

Power Words Review

Look at the words below. Circle any that you think you may know. Be ready to tell the class what the word means. Try to use the word in a sentence to show its meaning.

comrade	imbecile	operator	sinister
contraband	junk	oversee	skyward
counteract	lengthen	overspend	terrain
deluded	midsummer	quicken	trustworthy
disintegrated	midtown	ruler	uninhabited
idiotic	musician	seaworthy	warlike

Part 1: Context Clues

Remember that you can often figure out the meaning of an unknown word from the words that appear nearby. The words or phrases that surround an unknown word are called **context clues.**

A. Use context clues to figure out the meaning of the **boldfaced** word. Darken in the circle with the correct definition.

1. My **comrades** have stood by me for years and taken care of me during hard times.
   - ○ bosses
   - ○ pets
   - ○ friends
   - ○ enemies

2. Just because you do stupid things doesn't mean you're an **imbecile**.
   - ○ idiot
   - ○ worker
   - ○ genius
   - ○ slave

3. The farm is on a beautiful **terrain** of rolling hills and flowing streams.
   - ○ planet
   - ○ countryside
   - ○ block
   - ○ town

4. The old house had been **uninhabited** for years with no one to take care of it.
   - ○ without electricity
   - ○ without water
   - ○ without people
   - ○ without paint

Name _____ Date _____

Part 2: Multiple-Meaning Words

The word *multiple* means many. **Multiple-meaning words** are words that have more than one meaning.

A. Read each sentence below. Think about how the **boldfaced** word in the sentence is used. Then read the different meanings of that word below. Write the letter of the definition in the blank that matches the meaning of the boldfaced word in the sentence.

_____1. The thief was quite an **operator,** forcing people into giving them stuff.
    a. a person who operates a machine
    b. a person who gets what they want through illegal or mean ways

_____2. Ahmed saw a famous **star** when she visited California.
    a. a celebrity or famous person
    b. a heavenly body made up of burning gases

_____3. My favorite jacket has lost a **button** and I can't keep it closed.
    a. a switch that is pushed
    b. a round object used to fasten the parts of clothing together

_____4. Every Sunday we go to a **service** at our church.
    a. a branch of the armed forces, for example, the navy or army
    b. a religious ceremony
    c. a favor, often in return for something

_____5. The climber nearly **froze** to death when he became lost up in the cold mountains.
    a. stopped
    b. became frozen due to very low temperatures

_____6. I borrowed Carl's **ruler** to see how long the table was.
    a. a stick used to measure things
    b. the person in charge of a land, such as a king

_____7. My dad was very **cross** with me when I got a speeding ticket.
    a. an upright post with a piece at a right angle across it
    b. to be angry
    c. to pass from one side to another

_____8. My grandpa gets very tired of climbing each of the **steps** in his tall house.
    a. a manner of walking
    b. stairs

Part 3: Affixes and Base Words

A **base word** is a word that can stand alone. An **affix** is a word part added to the beginning or end of a base word. **Prefixes** and **suffixes** are affixes. Review the meaning of the following affixes until you can remember what each means.

> **counter-** means "opposite" or "contrary" / **over-** means "above" or "superior"
> **circum-** mean "around" / **contra-** means "opposed" or "against"
> **mid-** means "halfway" / **-ward** means "toward" / **-en** means "to become"
> **-like** mean "similar to" or "like" / **-worthy** means "safe for" or "suitable"
> **-ician** means "person who does something"

A. Match the meaning of the word in **Column A** with its definition in **Column B**. Break the words into their affixes and base words to help you. Use a dictionary if necessary.

Column A	Column B
1. _____ musician	A. in an attacking manner; similar to war
2. _____ seaworthy	B. someone able to be trusted; reliable
3. _____ midsummer	C. an argument against someone else's ideas
4. _____ oversee	D. to make longer
5. _____ skyward	E. to spend more than is allowed
6. _____ quicken	F. safe for sailing on the sea
7. _____ warlike	G. to sail or navigate around something
8. _____ contraband	H. a person who plays music
9. _____ midtown	I. halfway through the summer
10. _____ counteract	J. to watch over or manage
11. _____ overspend	K. towards the sky or heavens
12. _____ lengthen	L. illegal goods brought in or sold away
13. _____ trustworthy	M. to become faster
14. _____ counterargument	N. a part of town near the city center
15. _____ circumnavigate	O. to act against another

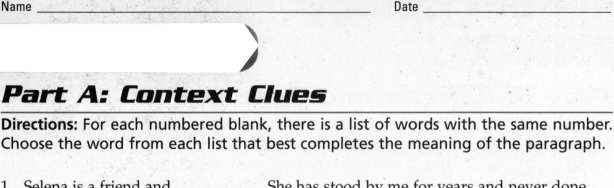

Part A: Context Clues

Directions: For each numbered blank, there is a list of words with the same number. Choose the word from each list that best completes the meaning of the paragraph.

1. Selena is a friend and _____. She has stood by me for years and never done
   (1)
   anything evil or _____.
   (2)

   1.   ○ enemy   2.   ○ sinister
         ○ boss   ○ skyward
         ○ comrade   ○ friendly
         ○ operator   ○ nice

2. Matt is not an _____. However, he does do very stupid and _____ things
   (3)   (4)
   once in a while.

   3.   ○ operator   4.   ○ great
         ○ imbecile   ○ contraband
         ○ artist   ○ idiotic
         ○ actor   ○ weary

3. The house is _____. No one lives there because it is located in dry and ugly
   (5)
   _____.
   (6)

   5.   ○ deluded   6.   ○ terrain
         ○ charming   ○ skyward
         ○ new   ○ planet
         ○ uninhabited   ○ tower

4. Maria was _____ by the builder. When she bought the house, she had no idea he
   (7)
   would _____ the old parts into small pieces and build anew.
   (8)

   7.   ○ trustworthy   8.   ○ lengthen
         ○ beaten   ○ disintegrate
         ○ deluded   ○ sell
         ○ fed   ○ build

Unit 6, Test

Part B: Multiple-Meaning Words

Directions: Read each sentence below. Find the word that fits in both sentences.

1. The pilot had to _____ the raging river.

   I was _____ with my little brother when he broke my model.

   ○ swim
   ○ cross
   ○ mad
   ○ furious

2. I got lost in the _____ of the jungle and couldn't find the trail.

   Lance has shown so much _____ in all of his school subjects.

   ○ work
   ○ vines
   ○ growth
   ○ time

3. Thomas pushed the _____ to start the elevator.

   My jacket is missing a _____ and I can't close it properly.

   ○ snap
   ○ starter
   ○ switch
   ○ button

4. My uncle was willing to _____ in the army.

   Mom will _____ dinner to everyone in the dining room.

   ○ cook
   ○ serve
   ○ join
   ○ fight

5. My dog loves to go running out in the _____.

   The new mall is now _____ for business.

   ○ ready
   ○ field
   ○ pasture
   ○ open

Unit 6, Test

Part C: Affixes and Base Words

Directions: Match the word in **Column A** with its definition in **Column B.** Write the letter of the correct definition in the blank provided.

Column A

1. _____ counterargument
2. _____ trustworthy
3. _____ warlike
4. _____ oversee
5. _____ lengthen
6. _____ contraband
7. _____ musician
8. _____ skyward
9. _____ circumnavigate
10. _____ midsummer

Column B

A. able to be trusted

B. a person who plays music

C. to watch over or manage

D. halfway through summer

E. toward the sky or heavens

F. an argument against someone else's ideas

G. to sail or navigate around something

H. in a hostile or attacking manner; similar to war

I. to make longer

J. illegal goods brought in or sold away

Directions: Match the affix in **Column A** with its meaning in **Column B.** Use the words above to help you decide the correct answer.

Column A

1. _____ over-
2. _____ -ward
3. _____ circum-
4. _____ mid-
5. _____ -ician
6. _____ -like
7. _____ contra-
8. _____ -worthy

Column B

A. a person who does something

B. halfway

C. safe for or suitable

D. similar to; like

E. opposed; against

F. above; superior

G. around

H. toward

Power Words

Look at the words below. Circle any that you think you may know. Be ready to tell the class what the word means. Also tell the class how you think you know that word.

barbarian	gladiator	rewired	unbreakable
clearing	preprinted	savage	unearthly
essential	replaceable	suspiciously	willful

Part 1: Structural Analysis

A **base word** is a word that can stand alone. An **affix** is a word part added to the beginning or ending of a base word. A **prefix** is an affix added to the beginning of a base word. A **suffix** is an affix added to the end of a base word. Study the meaning of the following affixes until you can remember what each means.

Affix	Meaning	Example
the prefix *pre-*	means *before*	prepay
the prefix *un-*	means *not* or *opposite of*	untie
the prefix *re-*	means *again* or *back*	replay
the suffix *-d* or *-ed*	makes a verb past tense	washed
the suffix *-able* or *-ible*	means *able to be*	playable
the suffix *-ly*	tells how something is done	loudly

A. The words below contain a prefix, a base word, and a suffix. Draw a line between the three parts of the word. Then write a definition on the blank. Use a dictionary if needed.

1. unbreakable: _____

2. unearthly: _____

3. replaceable: _____

4. preprinted: _____

5. rewired: _____

6. unlovely: _____

7. presoaked: _____

Unit 7, Lesson 1

Part 2: Syllabication

A **syllable** is a word part with one vowel sound. Remember that the vowels are the letters *a, e, i, o, u*, and sometimes *y*. All other letters are consonants. As a reminder, the chart below shows you the long and short vowel sounds.

Vowel	Long Sound	Short Sound
a	"a" as in day	"a" as in cat
e	"e" as in be	"e" as in set
i	"i" as in lie	"i" as in sit
o	"o" as in low	"o" as in hot
u	"u" as in blue	"u" as in bug

If you break an unknown word into syllables, it may help you figure out what the word means. Look at the rules below to see the correct places to divide words into syllables.

1. *war • plane* (between two words of a compound word)
2. *dis • arm* or *try • ing* (between a base word and a prefix or suffix)
3. *cor • rect* (between double consonants)
4. *clus • ter* (between two consonants, with vowels both before and after)
5. *be • hind* (<u>before</u> a single consonant if the vowel before it has a <u>long</u> sound)
6. *nev • er* (<u>after</u> a single consonant if the vowel before it has a <u>short</u> sound)

A. Circle the correct way to divide each word into syllables. Use a dictionary if needed.

1. homemade   A. hom • emade   B. home • made

2. suffer   A. su • ffer   B. suf • fer

3. hunger   A. hung • er   B. hun • ger

4. brightly   A. bright • ly   B. bri • ghtly

5. finish   A. fi • nish   B. fin • ish

6. airplane   A. airp • lane   B. air • plane

7. creeping   A. creep • ing   B. cre • eping

8. pilot   A. pi • lot   B. pil • ot

Part 3: Context Clues

When you come to a word that you don't know, read the words near the unknown word carefully. These words may give you **context clues** that help you figure out what the unknown word means. One type of context clue is a **definition** or **restatement clue.** This type of clue tells the exact meaning of an unknown word. For example, in the sentences below you see that the definition of *irritating* means "to make someone mad."

My friend is irritating me. She is really making me mad.

A. Look for definition clues. Write the definition of each **boldfaced** word on the line.

1. In order for the boy to be able to kill something, it was necessary, or **essential,** that he have a weapon.

   Essential means_____.

2. The boy no longer trusted his friend. He watched him **suspiciously.**

   Suspiciously means _____.

3. The animals gathered in the open **clearing** where there were no trees.

   Clearing means _____.

4. All the animals lived happily together. They had no problems and were **content.**

   Content means _____.

5. The king's ancestors had been **barbarians**—brutal people who killed and stole from others.

   Barbarians means _____.

6. **Gladiators,** men chosen to fight each other in front of others, were a favorite form of entertainment among the ancient people.

   Gladiator means _____.

7. To face a tiger was terrifying. The tiger is a wild, powerful, and **savage** beast.

   Savage means _____.

8. The young princess was as **willful** as her father. She always wanted to get her way.

   Willful means _____.

Power Words

Look at the words below. Circle any that you think you may know. Be ready to tell the class what the word means. Also tell the class how you think you know that word.

ably	disapproving	multitasking	surplus
brooch	displeased	omelet	survey
decade	malformed	studio	tuition

Part 1: Structural Analysis

A **base word** is a word that can stand alone. An **affix** is a word part added to the beginning or ending of a base word. A **prefix** is an affix added to the beginning of a base word. A **suffix** is an affix added to the end of a base word. Study the meaning of the following affixes until you can remember what each means.

Affix	Meaning	Example
the prefix **dis-**	means **not** or **lack of** or **away from**	<u>dis</u>agree
the prefix **multi-**	means **many**	<u>multi</u>fold
the prefix **mal-**	means **bad**	<u>mal</u>practice
the suffix **-d** or **-ed**	makes a verb past tense	brush<u>ed</u>
the suffix **-ing**	shows an on-going action	play<u>ing</u>
the suffix **-er** or **-or**	someone who does something	talk<u>er</u>

A. The words below contain a prefix, a base word, and a suffix. Draw a line between the three parts of the word. Then write a definition on the blank. Use a dictionary if needed.

1. maladjusted: _____

2. displeased: _____

3. multitasking: _____

4. displacer: _____

5. multicolored: _____

6. malformed: _____

7. disapproving: _____

Part 2: Syllabication

A **syllable** is a word part with one vowel sound. If you break an unknown word into syllables, it may help you figure out what the word means. Look at the examples below to see the correct places to divide words into syllables. Remember that the vowels are the letters *a, e, i, o, u,* and sometimes *y.* All other letters are consonants.

1. *fire • place* (between two words of a compound word)
2. *un • do* or *quick • ly* (between a base word and a prefix or suffix)
3. *mus • ter* (between two consonants, with vowels both before and after)
4. *de • cide* (<u>before</u> a single consonant if the vowel before it has a <u>long</u> sound)
5. *nev • er* (<u>after</u> a single consonant if the vowel before it has a <u>short</u> sound)
6. *big • ger* (between double consonants)

A. Circle the correct way to divide each word into syllables. Use a dictionary if needed.

1. unfriendly   A. un • friend • ly   B. unfri • end • ly

2. lumpy   A. lum • py   B. lu • mpy

3. corkscrew   A. cor • kscrew   B. cork • screw

4. rabbit   A. ra • bbit   B. rab • bit

5. petal   A. pe • tal   B. pet • al

B. Fluency: Practice reading the paragraph below until you can read it smoothly. The number in parentheses tell you how many syllables are in the underlined word. Draw diagonal lines (/) in the word to divide the syllables.

The mean king put anyone on trial who had made a <u>mistake</u> (2). He tried a person whether he was guilty or <u>innocent</u> (3). The king had a most unusual way of <u>putting</u> (2) a person on trial. He kept a <u>tiger</u> (2) waiting behind one of two doors. This hungry tiger was eager to tear people <u>apart</u> (2). A <u>person</u> (2) had to choose which door to open. The tiger listened for the person's <u>footsteps</u> (2). Often the poor man chose the wrong door and would try to shut it <u>quickly</u> (2). The people watching closed their <u>eyelids</u> (2). A <u>woman</u> (2) screamed as the tiger sprang out. Who would win, the man or the tiger?

Part 3: Context Clues

When you come to a word that you don't know, read the words near the unknown word carefully. These words may give you **context clues** that help you figure out what the unknown word means. One type of context clue is a **definition** or **restatement** **clue.** This type of clue tells the exact meaning of an unknown word. For example, in the sentences below you see that the definition of *irritating* means "to make someone mad."

My friend is irritating me. She is really making me mad.

A. Look for definition clues. Write the definition of each **boldfaced** word on the line.

1. My dad buys a new car every **decade,** or ten years.

   Decade means _____.

2. We had an **omelet** for breakfast. It was eggs filled with bacon and other stuff.

   Omelet means _____.

3. The painter worked in his **studio,** or artist's workroom, all night long.

   Studio means _____.

4. Kim loved jewelry and had an expensive gold **brooch** pinned to her coat.

   Brooch means _____.

5. The **tuition,** or cost to go to some colleges, can be very expensive.

   Tuition means _____.

6. The gladiator **ably** and skillfully beat the other fighter.

   Ably means _____.

7. My dad bought too many games. We didn't know what to do with the extra amount or **surplus.**

   Surplus means _____.

8. The mechanic will **survey** the engine. After he inspects it he will tell us what's wrong.

   Survey means _____.

Copyright © McDougal Littell Inc.

Power Words Review

Look at the words below. Circle any that you think you may know. Be ready to tell the class what the word means. Try to use the word in a sentence to show its meaning.

ably	displeased	preprinted	survey
barbarian	essential	replaceable	suspiciously
brooch	gladiator	rewired	tuition
clearing	malformed	savage	unbreakable
decade	multitasking	studio	unearthly
disapproving	omelet	surplus	willful

Part 1: Structural Analysis

A **base word** is a word that can stand alone. An **affix** is a word part added to the beginning or ending of a base word. Study the meaning of the following affixes until you can remember what each means. Then do the exercises on the next page.

Affix	Meaning	Example
the prefix *pre-*	means *before*	<u>pre</u>pay
the prefix *un-*	means *not* or *opposite of*	<u>un</u>tie
the prefix *re-*	means *again* or *back*	<u>re</u>play
the prefix *dis-*	means *not* or *lack of* or *away from*	<u>dis</u>agree
the prefix *multi-*	means *many*	<u>multi</u>fold
the prefix *mal-*	means *bad*	<u>mal</u>practice
the suffix *-able* or *-ible*	means *able to be*	play<u>able</u>
the suffix *-ly*	tells how something is done	loud<u>ly</u>
the suffix *-d* or *-ed*	makes a verb past tense	brush<u>ed</u>
the suffix *-ing*	shows an on-going action	play<u>ing</u>
the suffix *-er* or *-or*	someone who does something	talk<u>er</u>

Unit 7, Lesson 3

Part 1: Structural Analysis *continued*

A. The words in **Column A** below contain a prefix, a base word, and a suffix. Draw a line between the three parts of the word. Then match the word to its definition in **Column B**. Write the correct letter in the blank provided.

Column A

1. _____ unbreakable

2. _____ displacer

3. _____ preprinted

4. _____ malformed

5. _____ unlovely

6. _____ multitasking

7. _____ replaceable

8. _____ disapproving

Column B

A. not pretty

B. able to be replaced or placed again

C. in a way that shows dislike

D. doing a number of things at once

E. to have been badly formed or made

F. someone who moves something

G. to have been printed before an event

H. not able to be broken

Part 2: Syllabication

A. A **syllable** is a word part with one vowel sound. Look at the following rules about dividing words into syllables. Decide which rule fits the word divided at the bottom of the page. Write the number of that rule in front of the word.

1. *war • plane* (between two words of a compound word)
2. *dis • arm* or *quick • ly* (between a base word and a prefix or suffix)
3. *clus • ter* (between two consonants, with vowels both before and after)
4. *be • fore* (<u>before</u> a single consonant if the vowel before it has a <u>long</u> sound)
5. *cor • rect* (between double consonants)
6. *nev • er* (<u>after</u> a single consonant if the vowel before it has a <u>short</u> sound)

1. _____ home • made

2. _____ suf • fer

3. _____ pet • al

4. _____ hun • ger

5. _____ bright • ly

6. _____ wo • man

Part 3: Context Clues

Remember that you can often figure out the meaning of an unknown word from the words that appear near by. The words or phrases that surround an unknown word are called **context clues.**

A. Use context clues to figure out the meaning of the **boldfaced** word. Darken in the circle with the correct definition.

1. My brother looked at me **suspiciously** when I handed him his empty wallet.
   - ○ nicely
   - ○ untrustingly
   - ○ happily
   - ○ madly

2. The **gladiator** entered the arena to face the enemy.
   - ○ fighter
   - ○ worker
   - ○ trainer
   - ○ athlete

3. Flour is an **essential** part of making a cake. You can't make a cake without it.
   - ○ old
   - ○ simple
   - ○ needed
   - ○ interesting

4. My parents pay more **tuition** for school every year.
   - ○ costs
   - ○ time
   - ○ work
   - ○ bills

5. The team had a **surplus** of players. There were so many some never got to play.
   - ○ team
   - ○ extra amount
   - ○ not enough
   - ○ busload

6. The commander came to **survey** his troops to make sure they were ready.
   - ○ fight
   - ○ yell at
   - ○ order
   - ○ inspect

Part A: Structural Analysis

Directions: First, draw a line between the prefix, base word, and suffix in each of the words in **Column A**. Then write the letter of the definition in **Column B** that matches that word in the blank provided.

Column A

1. _____ replaceable

2. _____ multicolored

3. _____ malformed

4. _____ presoaked

5. _____ unlovely

6. _____ displeased

7. _____ unearthly

8. _____ preprinted

9. _____ disapproving

10. _____ displacer

11. _____ rewired

12. _____ maladjusted

13. _____ unbreakable

14. _____ multitasking

Column B

A. not able to be broken

B. not of the earth; unreal

C. to have been badly formed or made

D. to have printed before other materials

E. to have been badly adjusted or unable to fit in

F. many-colored

G. someone who sets or places things elsewhere

H. to have wired something again

I. able to be replace or placed again

J. not pretty

K. to be doing many jobs or tasks at once

L. to not have been pleased

M. to not be accepting or approving of something

N. to have soaked something earlier

Unit 7, Test

Part B: Syllabication

Directions: Separate the following words into syllables. Write the syllables on the lines.

1. lumpy   =   _____ + _____

2. rabbit   =   _____ + _____

3. unfriendly =   _____ + _____ + _____

4. hunger   =   _____ + _____

5. finish   =   _____ + _____

6. homemade   =   _____ + _____

7. cable   =   _____ + _____

8. powerful   =   _____ + _____ + _____

9. woman   =   _____ + _____

10. innocent   =   _____ + _____ + _____

11. petal   =   _____ + _____

12. apart   =   _____ + _____

13. defenseless =   _____ + _____ + _____

14. mistake   =   _____ + _____

15. footsteps   =   _____ + _____

16. intently   =   _____ + _____ + _____

17. corkscrew   =   _____ + _____

18. brightly   =   _____ + _____

19. suffer   =   _____ + _____

20. airplane   =   _____ + _____

Unit 7, Test

Part C: Context Clues

Directions: For each numbered blank, there is a list of words with the same number. Choose the word from each list that best completes the meaning of the paragraph.

1. The enemy soldiers were _____. They rode into the open _____, killing
   (1)   (2)
   and destroying everything in their path.

   1.   ○ dead   **2.**   ○ brooch
            ○ cowards   ○ clearing
            ○ barbarians   ○ sky
            ○ ably   ○ decade

2. My father is very _____. He always gets what he wants so I'm sure he'll be able
   (3)
   to find the money to pay for my college _____.
                                             (4)

   3.   ○ mean   **4.**   ○ religion
            ○ suspiciously   ○ essential
            ○ willful   ○ tuition
            ○ sad   ○ place

3. I can't believe it's been as long as a _____. Has it really been ten years since
   (5)
   you last visited my artist's workplace or _____ .
                                              (6)

   5.   ○ survey   **6.**   ○ clearing
            ○ decade   ○ studio
            ○ record   ○ tuition
            ○ month   ○ painting

4. This man was a _____ warrior. As a wild and brutal fighter, few other
   (7)
   _____ would fight him in the arena before the crowds of people.
   (8)

   7.   ○ brooch   **8.**   ○ gladiators
            ○ coward   ○ students
            ○ ably   ○ merchants
            ○ savage   ○ omelets

Power Words

Look at the words below. Circle any that you think you may know. Be ready to tell the class what the word means. Also tell the class how you think you know that word.

cyclone	mechanic	politics	spar
deck	metropolis	psychic	steer
hull	policy	rudder	thermos

Part 1: Specialized Vocabulary

People who work in a special field, such as sports or science, use special words. They use a **specialized vocabulary** to talk about their subjects. For example, a coach might use the word **goal.** When you come across specialized vocabulary, look at the words and sentences around the special word to help you figure out its meaning.

A. Fluency: Practice reading the selection below until you can read it smoothly. In this selection you will find specialized vocabulary about types of ships. The specialized vocabulary is in **bold.** Underline the words in the sentence that tell you what each bold word means.

There have been many types of ships in history. One early wooden ship was the **Roman galley.** This ship used a large number of soldiers or slaves to power it. The ship used long **oars,** or wooden paddles, for power. It could take seven men to pull one oar.

In Southeast Asia, a common ship is the **Chinese junk.** This is a light, flat-bottomed ship with large sails. **Sails** are large pieces of cloth to catch the wind. The boat is controlled with a steering bar or **rudder** from the **deck,** or top surface, of the ship.

In the 1800s the **clipper** ship was invented. This wooden ship had two to four **masts,** or long wooden poles, that held large sails. The sails caught much wind so that the ship went very fast, or at a fast "clip." It carried people and goods across the oceans.

The clipper ship was replaced with the **steamship.** The steamship used an engine powered by boiling water, or steam, rather than the wind. One type of steamship was the **paddle-wheel boat.** On a paddle-wheeler, the steam pushed a large wheel of flat boards. This wheel revolved down into the water to push the ship forward.

One of the many modern ships used today is the **tanker.** The tanker is a very large metal boat with powerful engines. Most of the inside is empty space which is filled with oil, or petroleum. Because an oil spill in the ocean can kill many living things, many tankers today have double-thick sides and bottoms, or **hulls.**

Unit 8, Lesson 1

Part 2: Using a Dictionary

A **dictionary** contains an alphabetical listing of words. Much information is provided about each word, or **entry**. Dictionaries tell you how to pronounce a word, its part of speech, and its meaning. Dictionaries may also tell you the history of the word. It may also give synonyms, or words that mean almost the same thing. When you look up a word, use the context of what you are reading to help you choose the definition that makes the most sense.

A. In each of the sentences, one word is underlined. Find the word in the boxed dictionary entries below. Decide which meaning best matches the context, or ideas, in the sentence. Then write the part of speech and the definition on the lines provided.

	Part of Speech	Definition

1. The sailors lay on the <u>deck</u> of the large ship.   _____   _____

2. My dad always takes the <u>hull</u> off of the peanuts before eating them.   _____   _____

3. Boxers will <u>spar</u> with each other to practice for a fight.   _____   _____

4. The captain of the ship could <u>steer</u> it through the narrow canal.   _____   _____

5. Sam said if I pushed him again he would <u>deck</u> me.   _____   _____

6. The tanker had a double <u>hull</u> to prevent oil spills.   _____   _____

---

deck (dĕk) *n.* **1.** A platform that goes from one side of a ship to another. **2.** A roofless area that is connected to a house; a porch. **3.** A pack of playing cards. *v. Slang.* **1.** To knock down with force.

hull (hŭl) *n.* **1.** The dry outer covering of a seed, fruit, or nut. **2.** The frame or body of a ship. **3.** The outer covering of a rocket or missile.

spar 1 (spär) *n.* **1.** A wooden or metal pole used to support a sail on a boat.
spar 2 (spär) *v.* **1.** To make boxing motions as if to hit someone.
spar 3 (spär) *n.* **1.** A light-colored mineral with a shiny luster.

steer 1 (stîr) *v.* **1.** To guide a vehicle or a vessel.
steer 2 (stîr) *n.* **2.** A young ox raised for beef.

Part 3: Greek and Latin Roots

Many English words are made up of word parts from other languages, especially Greek and Latin. These word parts are called **roots.** A root cannot stand alone, but knowing its meaning helps you figure out the meaning of the whole word. A group of words with the same root is called a **word family.** Study the chart of Greek roots below.

Root	Meaning	Example
psych	mind, soul, spirit	<u>psych</u>ic
poli	city	<u>poli</u>ce
cycl	circle, ring	bi<u>cycl</u>e
therm	heat	<u>therm</u>ometer
mech	machine	<u>mech</u>anical

A. Underline the root of each word in **Column A.** Then match each word with its correct meaning in **Column B.** Write the letter of the correct meaning in the space provided. Use a dictionary if necessary.

Column A

1. _____ metropolis
2. _____ tricycle
3. _____ mechanic
4. _____ psychotic
5. _____ thermos
6. _____ politics
7. _____ mechanize
8. _____ cyclone
9. _____ thermal
10. _____ policy

Column B

A. a self-propelled vehicle with three wheels

B. a container for keeping liquids warm

C. a tornado

D. the art or science of governing others

E. a person who works on machines

F. a city

G. a plan or course of action

H. to produce by machines

I. relating to or causing heat

J. a person with a mental illness

Power Words

Look at the words below. Circle any that you think you may know. Be ready to tell the class what the word means. Also tell the class how you think you know that word.

buckle	earthquake	flexible	scribble
crust	eject	project	scripture
dictate	fault	reflect	visual

Part 1: Specialized Vocabulary

Remember that people who work in a special field, such as sports, use special words. They use a **specialized vocabulary** to talk about their subjects. For example, a car racer might use the words **finish line.** When you come across specialized vocabulary, look at the words and sentences around the special word to help you figure out its meaning.

A. The following sentences have specialized vocabulary about earthquakes. The specialized vocabulary is in **bold.** Underline the words in the sentence that tell you what each bold word means. Then write a definition on the line. Use a dictionary if necessary.

1. The outer layer of the earth on which we live, or **crust,** is very thin.

   meaning: _____

2. A shaking of the earth's surface caused by a quick movement of the earth's crust is called an **earthquake.**

   meaning: _____

3. The earth's crust is split into giant sections. The places where these sections meet are called **faults.**

   meaning: _____

4. Every earthquake has an **epicenter**—the place on the earth's surface directly above where the earthquake originated.

   meaning: _____

5. People who study earthquakes are called **seismologists.** This word comes from the Greek word *seismos,* which means "to shake."

   meaning: _____

6. Earthquakes can cause **tsunamis**—large sea waves that can cause great damage.

   meaning: _____

Unit 8, Lesson 2

Part 2: Using a Dictionary

A **dictionary** contains an alphabetical listing of words. Much information is provided about each word, or **entry.** Dictionaries tell you how to pronounce a word, its part of speech, and its meaning. Dictionaries may also tell you the history of the word. It may also give synonyms, or words that mean almost the same thing. When you look up a word, use the context of what you are reading to help you choose the definition that makes the most sense.

A. In each of the sentences, one word is underlined. Find the word in the boxed dictionary entries below. Decide which meaning best matches the context, or ideas, in the sentence. Then write the part of speech and the definition on the lines provided.

	Part of Speech	Definition
1. The bread was so dry that the <u>crust</u> was stiff as a board.	_____	_____
2. Jamie stole the apple so he is the one at <u>fault</u>.	_____	_____
3. The earthquake off the coast of Japan caused a huge tidal <u>wave</u>.	_____	_____
4. During an earthquake the top layer of the earth can <u>buckle</u>.	_____	_____
5. The limbs of the tree out back always <u>wave</u> in the wind.	_____	_____
6. David had a terrible <u>fault</u> in that he told too many lies.	_____	_____

---

buck•le (bŭk′ el) *n.* **1.** A clasp for closing two ends of a belt. *v.* **1.** To cause to bend or fold, or warp. **2.** To apply oneself with determination. **buckle down.**

crust (krŭst) *n.* **1.** The hard outer part of bread. **2.** A hard covering or surface. **3.** The outer layer of the earth's surface.

fault 1 (fŏlt) *n.* **1.** A weakness in one's personality or character. **2.** A weakness or mistake. **3.** A break or fracture in a rock.—**idioms. at fault. 1.** To be guilty or in error. **find fault. 2.** To criticize or blame someone.

wave (wāv) *v.* **1.** To move freely up and down or back and forth, as branches in the wind. **2.** To make a signal with one's hand. *n.* **1.** A ridge or swell moving through the surface of a body of water. **2.** A sudden great rise.

Unit 8, Lesson 2

Part 3: Greek and Latin Roots

Many English words are made up of word parts from other languages, especially Greek and Latin. These word parts are called **roots**. A root cannot stand alone, but knowing its meaning helps you figure out the meaning of the whole word. A group of words with the same root is called a **word family.** Study the chart of **Latin** roots below.

Root	Meaning	Example
ject	throw, hurl	eject
vid, vis	see	vision
dic, dict	speak, say, tell	dictate
flect, flex	bend	reflect
scrib, script	write	scripture

A. Underline the root of each word in **Column A.** Then match each word with its correct meaning in **Column B.** Write the letter of the correct meaning in the space provided. Use a dictionary if necessary.

Column A

1. _____ video

2. _____ dictionary

3. _____ flexible

4. _____ eject

5. _____ scribble

6. _____ project

7. _____ dictate

8. _____ reflect

9. _____ scripture

10. _____ visual

Column B

A. able to be bent

B. to have someone write down your speech

C. to thrust outward or forward

D. sacred writings

E. to throw or bend back light or an image

F. seen or able to be seen by the eye

G. a book containing word meanings

H. to write quickly

I. to throw out forcefully

J. the visual part of a TV broadcast

Power Words Review

Look at the words below. Circle any that you think you may know. Be ready to tell the class what the word means. Also tell the class how you think you know that word.

buckle	eject	policy	scribble
crust	fault	politics	scripture
cyclone	flexible	project	spar
deck	hull	psychic	steer
dictate	mechanic	reflect	thermos
earthquake	metropolis	rudder	visual

Part 1: Specialized Vocabulary

Remember that people who work in a special field, such as sports or science, use special words. They use a **specialized vocabulary** to talk about their subjects.

A. In Lesson 1 you learned some of the specialized words for different types of ships. Pictured below are the ships described in Lesson 1. See if you can match the picture to the correct name of the ship. Write the correct letter in the space provided.

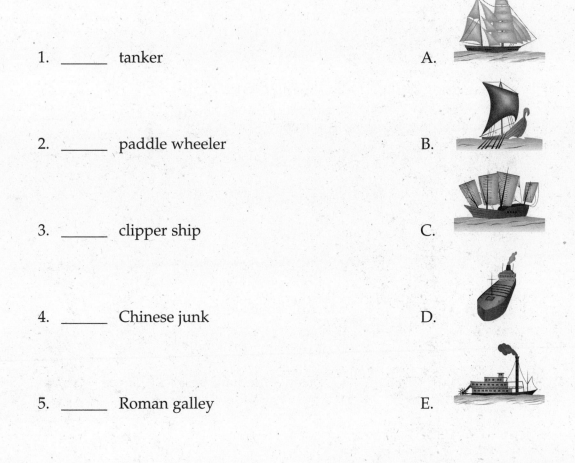

1. _____ tanker   A.

2. _____ paddle wheeler   B.

3. _____ clipper ship   C.

4. _____ Chinese junk   D.

5. _____ Roman galley   E.

Name _____ Date _____

Part 2: Using a Dictionary

A **dictionary** contains an alphabetical listing of words. Much information is provided about each word, or **entry**. Dictionaries tell you how to pronounce a word, its part of speech, and its meaning. At the top of each page of a dictionary are two **guide words** in **boldface** letters. These words tell you the <u>first</u> and <u>last</u> word on that page. When looking up a word, use the guide words to find the correct page. The word you are looking up should come between the two guide words alphabetically, or in ABC order.

A. In **Column A** are words you have had in this unit. In **Column B** are sets of guide words. Decide between which two sets of guide words each of the words in Column A will fall. Write the letter of the correct answer on the blank provided.

Column A

1. _____ crust
2. _____ cyclone
3. _____ deck
4. _____ dictate
5. _____ fault
6. _____ flexible
7. _____ mechanic
8. _____ metropolis
9. _____ politics
10. _____ project
11. _____ reflect
12. _____ rudder
13. _____ scribble
14. _____ steer
15. _____ visual

Column B

A. metro – Miami
B. fleece – flight
C. dicey – die
D. crud – crustacean
E. screwball – scrub
F. referee – reform
G. viscount – vital
H. decency – declare
I. ruckus – rule
J. stay – stem
K. fatal – fax
L. police – polka
M. cuttlebone – czar
N. progress – prolong
O. mean – median

Copyright © McDougal Littell Inc.

Part 3: Greek and Latin Roots

Remember that many English words are made up of word parts from other languages, especially Greek and Latin. Study the chart of **Greek** and **Latin** roots below.

Root	Meaning	Example
psych	mind, soul, spirit	psychic
poli	city	police
cycl	circle, ring	bicycle
therm	heat	thermometer
mech	machine	mechanical
ject	throw, hurl	eject
vid, vis	see	vision
dic, dict	speak, say, tell	dictate
flect, flex	bend	reflect
scrib, script	write	scripture

A. Match the root in **Column A** with its correct meaning in **Column B**. Write the letter of the correct meaning in the space provided. Use a dictionary if necessary.

Column A

1. _____ metropolis

2. _____ eject

3. _____ mechanic

4. _____ flexible

5. _____ thermos

6. _____ politics

7. _____ scripture

8. _____ cyclone

Column B

A. to throw out forcefully

B. a container for keeping liquids warm

C. a tornado

D. the art or science of governing others

E. a person who works on machines

F. a city

G. able to be bent

H. sacred writings

Part A: Specialized Vocabulary

Directions: The words in the following list belong to one of the two specialized vocabulary groups at the bottom of the page. Write each word under its correct label.

clipper	tanker	epicenter
seismologists	hull	fault
steamship	crust	tsunamis
rudder	deck	junk

Category A: Ships

_____   _____   _____

_____   _____   _____

_____   _____

Category A: Earthquakes

_____   _____   _____

_____   _____   _____

Directions: Match the specialized vocabulary word in **Column A** with its correct definition in **Column B.** Write the correct letter in the blank provided.

Column A

1. _____ masts

2. _____ tsunami

3. _____ galley

4. _____ deck

5. _____ paddle-wheeler

6. _____ crust

7. _____ oars

8. _____ fault

Column B

A. a long paddle used to propel a boat forward

B. the top layer of the earth's surface

C. long poles which hold the sails on a ship

D. a steamship propelled by a revolving wheel

E. a break or fracture in rock

F. a large tidal wave

G. the platform that spreads across a ship's surface

H. an ancient ship powered by men pulling oars

Unit 8, Test

Part B: Using a Dictionary

Directions: In each of the sentences, one word is underlined. Find the word in the boxed dictionary entries below. Decide which meaning best matches the context, or ideas, in the sentence. Write the part of speech and the definition on the lines provided.

	Part of Speech	Definition

1. A hole was punched in the <u>hull</u> of the ship during the storm.   _____   _____

2. The <u>crust</u> of the earth can rip apart during an earthquake.   _____   _____

3. The <u>spar</u> on the sailboat was broken.   _____   _____

4. The sails of the ship were repaired on the <u>deck</u>.   _____   _____

5. A long rudder is used to <u>steer</u> a Chinese junk.   _____   _____

---

buck le (bŭk′ el) *n.* **1.** A clasp for closing two ends of a belt. *v.* **1.** To cause to bend or fold, or warp. **2.** To apply oneself with determination. **buckle down.**

crust (krŭst) *n.* **1.** The hard outer part of bread. **2.** A hard covering or surface. **3.** The outer layer of the earth's surface.

deck (dĕk) *n.* **1.** A platform that goes from one side of a ship to another. **2.** A roofless area that is connected to a house; a porch. **3.** A pack of playing cards. *v. Slang.* **1.** To knock down with force.

fault (fŏlt) *n.* **1.** A weakness in one's personality or character. **2.** A weakness or mistake. **3.** A break or fracture in a rock.—**idioms. at fault. 1.** To be guilty or in error. **find fault. 2.** To criticize or blame someone.

hull (hŭl) *n.* **1.** The dry outer covering of a seed, fruit, or nut. **2.** The frame or body of a ship. **3.** The outer covering of a rocket or missile.

spar 1 (spär) *n.* **1.** A wooden or metal pole used to support a sail on a boat.
spar 2 (spär) *v.* **1.** To make boxing motions as if to hit someone.
spar 3 (spär) *n.* **1.** A light-colored mineral with a shiny luster.

steer 1 (stîr) *v.* **1.** To guide a vehicle or a vessel.
steer 2 (stîr) *n.* **2.** A young ox raised for beef.

Unit 8, Test

Part C: Greek and Latin Roots

Directions: Match the meaning of the word in **Column B** with the word in **Column A.**
Fill in the letter of the definition on the blank provided.

1. _____ scripture   A. a city

2. _____ mechanic   B. to throw out forcefully

3. _____ video   C. to write quickly

4. _____ cyclone   D. sacred writing

5. _____ policy   E. a person who works on machines

6. _____ eject   F. a tornado

7. _____ scribble   G. a container for keeping liquids warm

8. _____ thermos   H. to throw back or bend light or an image

9. _____ reflect   I. a plan or course of action

10. _____ flexible   J. the art or science of governing others

11. _____ metropolis   K. able to be bent

12. _____ politics   L. the visual part of a TV broadcast

Directions: Each Latin and Greek root below has two definitions written beside it.
Only one is correct. Write the letter of the correct one on the blank provided.

1. _____ cycle   A. circle, ring   B. bend

2. _____ vid, vis   A. mind, soul   B. see

3. _____ poli   A. write   B. city

4. _____ scrib, script A. heat   B. write

5. _____ therm   A. machine   B. heat

6. _____ dic, dict   A. speak, say, tell B. city

7. _____ psych   A. mind, soul   B. throw

8. _____ ject   A. see   B. throw

Power Words

Look at the words below. Circle any that you think you may know. Be ready to tell the class what the word means. Also tell the class how you think you know that word.

adviser	biography	flight	optician
apprentice	chronological	humble	scales
bibliography	defy	moonlight	unlock

Part 1: Greek and Latin Roots

Many English words are made up of word parts from other languages, especially Greek and Latin. These word parts are called **roots**. A root cannot stand alone, but knowing its meaning helps you figure out the meaning of the whole word. A group of words with the same root is called a **word family**. Study the chart of **Greek** roots below.

Root	Meaning	Example
bio	life	<u>bio</u>logy
chron	time	<u>chron</u>ological
bibl, biblio	books	<u>bibl</u>e
opt	visible	<u>opt</u>ician
cardi	heart	<u>cardi</u>ac

A. Underline the root of each word in **Column A.** Then match each word with its correct meaning in **Column B.** Write the letter of the correct meaning in the space provided. Use a dictionary if necessary.

Column A

1. _____ optician

2. _____ biography

3. _____ cardiac arrest

4. _____ bibliography

5. _____ chronological

6. _____ biology

Column B

A. the science of the structure of life

B. one who makes lens and eyeglasses

C. a description of someone's life

D. a heart attack that stops the heart beat

E. a list or books or writings

F. arranged in time order

Part 2: Multiple-Meaning Words

The word *multiple* means many. **Multiple-meaning words** are words that have more than one meaning. For example, the word *fly* can mean to sail through the air. It can also be a type of insect.

A. Read each sentence below. Think about how the **bold** word in the sentence is used. Then read the different meanings of that word below. Write the letter of the definition in the blank that matches the meaning of the bold word in the sentence.

_____1. Chan the great carver would **stand** before the stone to study it.
　　　a. a booth or stall or counter to display goods
　　　b. to be upright on both feet

_____2. Sometimes the **rock** would speak to Chan.
　　　a. to move back and forth or from side to side
　　　b. a type of music
　　　c. a hard, natural mineral; a stone

_____3. Chan placed his **ear** to the stone to hear how it should be carved.
　　　a. the organ used for hearing
　　　b. the seed-bearing part of a cereal plant, such as corn

_____4. From **deep** inside the rock came a gentle sound.
　　　a. rich in color
　　　b. the ocean
　　　c. extending far below or within something

_____5. Chan heard a fish within the stone swimming among the **reeds.**
　　　a. one of a type of musical instruments, such as a clarinet
　　　b. tall grasses that grow in wet areas

_____6. Chan knew he could not carve a dragon with **scales.**
　　　a. an instrument for checking the weight of something
　　　b. a small platelike covering of fish

_____7. The king dragged Chan down a **flight** of steps when he saw his fish.
　　　a. the motion of an object through the air
　　　b. a scheduled airplane trip
　　　c. a series of stairs

_____8. However, when the king saw the carved fish by the **pool,** he loved them.
　　　a. a game played on a table with balls and a stick
　　　b. a small body of still water

Unit 9, Lesson 1

Part 3: Syllabication

A **syllable** is a word part with one vowel sound. If you break an unknown word into syllables, it may help you figure out what the word means. Look at the rules below to see the correct places to divide words into syllables. Remember that the vowels are the letters *a, e, i, o, u,* and sometimes *y.* All other letters are consonants.

1. *war • plane* (between two words of a compound word)

2. *dis • arm* or *quick • ly* (between a base word and a prefix or suffix)

3. *clus • ter* (between two consonants, with vowels both before and after)

4. *de • cide* (<u>before</u> a single consonant if the vowel before it has a <u>long</u> sound)

5. *cor • rect* (between double consonants)

6. *nev • er* (<u>after</u> a single consonant if the vowel before it has a <u>short</u> sound)

7. *peo • ple* (in words ending with a consonant + *-le,* divide the word before the consonant that comes before the *-le*)

A. Read each of the sentences below. On the blank provided, rewrite the underlined word into its syllables. Then write the number of the rule that tells how to divide a word.

1. The brave man decided to <u>defy</u> the king and went to war anyway.   **Rule(s)**

   _____ + _____   _____

2. The <u>humble</u> stone carver never bragged about how good he was.

   _____ + _____   _____

3. The young <u>apprentice</u> was on his third day of learning his new job.

   _____ + _____ + _____   _____ & _____

4. The fish carving was beautiful under the <u>moonlight</u>.

   _____ + _____   _____

5. The carver tried to <u>unlock</u> the beautiful creature inside each piece of rock.

   _____ + _____   _____

6. The king asked his <u>advisers</u> for help in making a decision.

   _____ + _____ + _____   _____ & _____

Power Words

Look at the words below. Circle any that you think you may know. Be ready to tell the class what the word means. Also tell the class how you think you know that word.

approve	defect	gracious	offend
audio	factory	junction	pigtails
cross	fragment	motionless	unfair

Part 1: Greek and Latin Roots

Many English words are made up of word parts from other languages, especially Greek and Latin. These word parts are called **roots.** A root cannot stand alone, but knowing its meaning helps you figure out the meaning of the whole word. A group of words with the same root is called a **word family.** Study the chart of **Latin** roots below.

Root	Meaning	Example
fract, frag	break	fragment
grat, grac	pleasing	gracious
fact, fect	do, make	factory
junct	join	junction
aud	hear	audio

A. Underline the root of each word in **Column A.** Then match each word with its correct meaning in **Column B.** Write the letter of the correct meaning in the space provided. Use a dictionary if necessary.

Column A

1. _____ junction

2. _____ gracious

3. _____ factory

4. _____ audio

5. _____ fragment

6. _____ defect

Column B

A. something made wrong or improperly

B. related to sound

C. a small, broken off piece

D. kind and warm; pleasing

E. a place where two things join

F. a place where things are made

Unit 9, Lesson 2

Part 2: Multiple-Meaning Words

The word *multiple* means many. **Multiple-meaning words** are words that have more than one meaning. For example, the word *fly* can mean to sail through the air. It can also be a type of insect.

A. Read each sentence below. Think about how the **bold** word in the sentence is used. Then read the different meanings of that word below. Write the letter of the definition in the blank that matches the meaning of the bold word in the sentence.

_____1. Rosaura's mother was **cross** that she wanted to go to her friend's house.
   a. an upright post with a piece near the top that goes across it
   b. angry

_____2. Rosaura explained to her mother that she had been invited to a **party.**
   a. a political group
   b. a gathering of people to have fun

_____3. Her mother told her that she was just the daughter of a **maid.**
   a. an unmarried girl
   b. a woman servant

_____4. She warned Rosaura not to **break** anything.
   a. a pause in an activity
   b. to cause to crumble into parts
   c. to make a sudden dash or run

_____5. At the party, Rosaura met a rude girl with a large **bow** in her hair.
   a. a weapon used to launch arrows
   b. a rod used to draw across the strings of a violin
   c. a knot having two loops and two ends

_____6. Rosaura helped the lady of the house **pass** out the slices of cake.
   a. to move ahead of another
   b. to die
   c. a permit or ticket
   d. to transfer from one to another

_____7. She also helped the magician pull cards out of the **pack.**
   a. a sturdy bag strapped to a person
   b. a complete set of related items
   c. a group of animals

_____8. However, the lady of the house tried to pay Rosaura when it was time to **leave.**
   a. to go away from a place
   b. official permission to be away from work

Unit 9, Lesson 2

Part 3: Syllabication

A **syllable** is a word part with one vowel sound. If you break an unknown word into syllables, it may help you figure out what the word means. Look at the rules below to see the correct places to divide words into syllables. Remember that the vowels are the letters *a, e, i, o, u,* and sometimes *y.* All other letters are consonants.

1. *war • plane* (between two words of a compound word)

2. *dis • arm* or *quick • ly* (between a base word and a prefix or suffix)

3. *clus • ter* (between two consonants, with vowels both before and after)

4. *be • hind* (<u>before</u> a single consonant if the vowel before it has a <u>long</u> sound)

5. *cor • rect* (between double consonants)

6. *nev • er* (<u>after</u> a single consonant if the vowel before it has a <u>short</u> sound)

7. *peo • ple* (in words ending with a consonant + *-le,* divide the word before the consonant that comes before the *-le*)

A. Read each of the sentences below. On the blank provided, rewrite the underlined word into its syllables. Then write the number of the rule that tells how to divide a word.

1. The young girl did not <u>approve</u> of the way her mother spoke.   **Rule (s)**

   _____ + _____   _____

2. Her mother thought it was a <u>terrible</u> idea that she decided to go.

   _____ + _____ + _____   _____ & _____

3. At first, the girl was <u>motionless</u> and couldn't do or say anthing.

   _____ + _____ + _____   _____ & _____

4. One of the girls at the party had <u>pigtails</u>.

   _____ + _____   _____

5. The girl didn't say anything bad to <u>offend</u> anyone.

   _____ + _____   _____

6. She thought it was <u>unfair</u> that she wasn't treated the same as everyone else.

   _____ + _____   _____

Power Words Review

Look at the words below. Circle any that you think you may know. Be ready to tell the class what the word means. Also tell the class how you think you know that word.

adviser	chronological	fragment	offend
apprentice	cross	gracious	optician
approve	defect	humble	pigtails
audio	defy	junction	scales
bibliography	factory	moonlight	unfair
biography	flight	motionless	unlock

Part 1: Greek and Latin Roots

Many English words are made up of word parts from other languages, especially Greek and Latin. These word parts are called **roots.** A root cannot stand alone, but knowing its meaning helps you figure out the meaning of the whole word. A group of words with the same root is called a **word family.** Study the chart of **Greek** and **Latin** roots below. Then do the exercise on the next page.

Root	Meaning	Example
bio	life	biology
chron	time	chronological
bibl, biblio	books	bible
opt	visible	optician
cardi	heart	cardiac
fract, frag	break	fragment
grat, grac	pleasing	gracious
fact, fect	do, make	factory
junct	join	junction
aud	hear	audio

Unit 9, Lesson 3

Part 1: Greek and Latin Roots continued

A. Match each word in **Column A** with its correct meaning in **Column B.** Write the letter of the correct meaning in the space provided. Use a dictionary if necessary.

Column A

1. _____ optician
2. _____ gracious
3. _____ fragment
4. _____ bibliography
5. _____ junction
6. _____ biology
7. _____ biography
8. _____ cardiac arrest
9. _____ audio
10. _____ chronological
11. _____ factory
12. _____ defect

Column B

A. the science of the structure of life

B. related to sound

C. a place where things are made

D. a heart attack that stops the heart beat

E. something made wrong or improperly

F. arranged in time order

G. kind and warm; pleasing

H. a description of someone's life

I. a small, broken off piece

J. one who makes lens and eyeglasses

K. a place where two things join

L. a list or books or writings

Part 2: Multiple-Meaning Words

The word *multiple* means many. **Multiple-meaning words** are words that have more than one meaning.

A. Fluency: Practice reading the paragraph below until you can read it smoothly. There are 12 multiple-meaning words from the last two lessons in the paragraph. Circle each one.

Louisa ran up the flight of stairs. She was so excited to be going to the party. She pulled the red dress out from deep in her closet and stuffed it into her pack. Running to the bathroom, she decided to stand on the scales to check her weight. Then she tied a bow in her hair. Meanwhile, her mother had her ear to the door. Her mother walked into Louisa's messy room. "Louisa," she said, "I'm not your maid. If you don't want me to be cross, clean up this room before you leave." Louisa said, "Oh Ma, give me a break!"

Unit 9, Lesson 3

Part 3: Syllabication

A **syllable** is a word part with one vowel sound. If you break an unknown word into syllables, it may help you figure out what the word means. Look at the rules below to see the correct places to divide words into syllables. Remember that the vowels are the letters *a, e, i, o, u,* and sometimes *y.* All other letters are consonants.

1. *war • plane* (between two words of a compound word)

2. *dis • arm* or *quick • ly* (between a base word and a prefix or suffix)

3. *clus • ter* (between two consonants, with vowels both before and after)

4. *be • fore* (<u>before</u> a single consonant if the vowel before it has a <u>long</u> sound)

5. *cor • rect* (between double consonants)

6. *nev • er* (<u>after</u> a single consonant if the vowel before it has a <u>short</u> sound)

7. *peo • ple* (in words ending with a consonant + *-le,* divide the word before the consonant that comes before the *-le*)

A. The words below have been divided into their syllables. Decide which rules from above were used to divide the words. In some cases, more than one rule was used. Write the number(s) of the rules in the blanks provided.

Syllables   **Rules**

1. moon / light   1. _____

2. un / lock   2. _____

3. of / fend   3. _____

4. hum / ble   4. _____

5. de / fy   5. _____

6. mo / tion / less   6. _____ _____

7. ap / prove   7. _____

8. ap / pren / tice   8. _____ _____

9. pig / tails   9. _____

10. ter / ri / ble   10. _____ _____

Part A: Greek and Latin Roots

Directions: Match the meaning of the word in **Column B** with the word in **Column A**. Fill in the letter of the definition on the blank provided.

Column A

1. _____ bibliography

2. _____ factory

3. _____ audio

4. _____ optician

5. _____ biology

6. _____ junction

7. _____ defect

8. _____ cardiac arrest

9. _____ fragment

10. _____ chronological

11. _____ gracious

12. _____ biography

Column B

A. the science of the structure of life

B. related to sound

C. a place where things are made

D. a heart attack that stops the heart beat

E. something made wrong or improperly

F. arranged in time order

G. kind and warm; pleasing

H. a description of someone's life

I. a small, broken off piece

J. one who makes lens and eyeglasses

K. a place where two things join

L. a list or books or writings

Directions: Each Latin and Greek root below has two definitions. Only one is correct. Write the letter of the correct one on the blank provided.

1. _____ bio | A. life | B. heart

2. _____ fact. fect | A. do, make | B. join

3. _____ chron | A. break | B. time

4. _____ junct | A. join | B. books

5. _____ bibl, biblio | A. visible | B. books

6. _____ opt | A. pleasing | B. visible

7. _____ grat, grac | A. heart | B. pleasing

8. _____ cardi | A. join | B. heart

Unit 9, Test

Part B: Multiple-Meaning Words

Directions: Read each sentence below. Find the word that fits in both sentences.

1. I will never_____ my math test.

   Sheila needed a _____ to go to the office.

   ○ break
   ○ stand
   ○ pass
   ○ permit

2. Kim ran up the _____ of stairs.

   My dad is coming in on a _____ from New York.

   ○ stand
   ○ pass
   ○ set
   ○ flight

3. We couldn't wait to go to the _____ after the game.

   My mom belongs to the Democratic _____.

   ○ party
   ○ pool
   ○ break
   ○ fundraiser

4. Juan's mom was _____ when he was late from school.

   There was a _____ atop the soldier's grave.

   ○ mad
   ○ cross
   ○ stone
   ○ reed

5. The dragon was covered in large, green _____.

   When my sister is on a diet, she refuses to go to the _____.

   ○ reeds
   ○ party
   ○ scales
   ○ bows

Unit 9, Test

Part C: Syllabication

Directions: Separate the following words into syllables. Write the syllables on the lines.

1. moonlight   =   _____ + _____

2. unlock   =   _____ + _____

3. terrible   =   _____ + _____ + _____

4. silence   =   _____ + _____

5. approve   =   _____ + _____

6. motionless   =   _____ + _____ + _____

7. pigtails   =   _____ + _____

8. defy   =   _____ + _____

9. unfair   =   _____ + _____

10. quickly   =   _____ + _____

11. apprentice   =   _____ + _____ + _____

12. offend   =   _____ + _____

13. people   =   _____ + _____

14. baseball   =   _____ + _____

15. humble   =   _____ + _____

16. cluster   =   _____ + _____

17. advisers   =   _____ + _____ + _____

18. never   =   _____ + _____

19. cable   =   _____ + _____

20. warplane   =   _____ + _____

Copyright © McDougal Littell Inc.

Power Words

Look at the words below. Circle any that you think you may know. Be ready to tell the class what the word means. Also tell the class how you think you know that word.

feat	pauper	rap	suite
flair	poll	recuperation	view
muddle	poverty	shudder	wealth

Part 1: Middle English Words

In the year 1066, England was defeated by the Normans, who were a people living in northern France. The Norman leader, William the Conqueror, became the ruler of England. As time went on, parts of the Norman language of French merged with Old English to form Middle English. It was not as harsh-sounding as Old English. Many Norman words had been borrowed from other languages, such as Latin and Greek.

A. The words in **Column A** show part of a word's **etymology,** or its origin. Look at the words closely. Then decide which modern Middle English word in **Column B** came from the original in **Column A**. Write the letter of the correct word in the blank.

Column A	Column B
1. _____ flairer (Old French)	A. poverty
2. _____ paupertas (Latin)	B. rap
3. _____ vewe (Middle English & Anglo-Norman)	C. right
4. _____ rappen (Middle English)	D. poll
5. _____ welthe (Middle English)	E. porpoise
6. _____ riht (Middle & Old English)	F. hall
7. _____ wrappen (Middle English)	G. wealth
8. _____ factum (Latin)	H. guest
9. _____ halle (Middle English)	I. flair
10. _____ pol (Middle English & Middle Dutch)	J. feat
11. _____ porc peis (Middle English & Old French)	K. view
12. _____ gest (Middle English)	L. wrap

Unit 10, Lesson 1

Part 2: Homophones

Words that sound the same but have different spellings and meanings are called **homophones**. For example, **role** and **roll** are homophones. Here are some other examples of homophones.

pole and **poll**	**flair** and **flare**	**feet** and **feat**
haul and **hall**	**rap** and **wrap**	**guessed** and **guest**
write and **right**	**reed** and **read**	**bred** and **bread**

A. Decide which of the homophones above answer the questions. Write the correct homophone in the blank. Use a dictionary if necessary.

1. What do you do to a present?   _____

2. What is something you light if you have an accident? _____

3. On what do you put shoes?   _____

4. If it isn't wrong, what is it?   _____

5. What is a plant that grows in lakes or rivers?   _____

6. At school, one shouldn't run in the what?   _____

7. What did you do if you didn't know the test answer? _____

8. When you are staying with someone, what are you?   _____

9. If you take a survey, you also take a what?   _____

10. How someone is raised is how someone is what?   _____

B. Circle the two homophones in each sentence.

1. Susan was on the way to see how much she would weigh.

2. We've been trying to weave a new rug for my mom.

3. I would have died if I had dyed my new white shirt purple.

4. Kim missed seeing the sign because of the mist on the car windshield.

5. My sister is so sweet sitting in her office suite all day long.

Unit 10, Lesson 1

Part 3: Shades of Meaning

Words may have small differences in meaning. A reader must know the exact meaning of a word to understand what the writer is saying. For example, a box that is *little* is different from a box that it is *tiny*. Tiny is much smaller than little.

A. Read the sentence with the missing word. Then read the question about the missing word. Choose the word that best answers the question.

1. The freezing wind made Maria _____ as we sat at the bus stop.

   Which of these words would indicate that Maria shivered or shook?

   A. stretch
   B. snuggle
   C. shudder
   D. relax

2. Kari would need a lot of time for _____ after her skateboard accident.

   Which of these words would indicate that Kim would need time for getting well?

   A. sleep
   B. recuperation
   C. vacation
   D. rest

3. A story from the Bible says that as a baby, Moses was hidden in the _____.

   Which of these words would indicate that Moses was hidden in marsh grass?

   A. swamp
   B. algae
   C. bushes
   D. reeds

4. Everything was just a _____ after the cat walked across the pieces of the puzzle.

   Which of these words would indicate that everything was mixed up?

   A. loss
   B. muddle
   C. model
   D. disaster

Power Words

Look at the words below. Circle any that you think you may know. Be ready to tell the class what the word means. Also tell the class how you think you know that word.

cinch	knight	ore	sole
grate	manner	pun	urn
inverted	manor	remnants	wail

Part 1: Middle English Words

Remember that many of our words come from Middle English. This was the language of England when the Normans from northern France conquered England. Many Norman words had been borrowed from other languages, such as Latin and Greek.

A. The words in **Column A** show part of a word's **etymology,** or its origin. Look at the words closely. Then decide which modern Middle English word in **Column B** came from the original in **Column A.** Write the letter of the correct word in the blank.

Column A

1. _____ urna (Latin)

2. _____ manoir (Middle English & Old French)

3. _____ wailen (Middle English)

4. _____ solea (Latin)

5. _____ manu (Middle English & Old English)

6. _____ ora (Middle English)

7. _____ graten (Middle English)

8. _____ stel (Middle English)

9. _____ hreol (Middle & Old English)

10. _____ cniht (Middle & Old English)

11. _____ sawol (Middle & Old English)

12. _____ niht (Middle & Old English)

Column B

A. wail

B. ore

C. soul

D. manor

E. grate

F. knight

G. steel

H. sole

I. manner

J. night

K. reel

L. urn

Unit 10, Lesson 2

Part 2: Homophones

Words that sound the same but have different spellings and meanings are called **homophones**. For example, **manor** and **manner** are homophones. Here are some other examples of homophones.

mane and **main**	**great** and **grate**	**night** and **knight**
wail and **whale**	**reel** and **real**	**steel** and **steal**
ore and **or**	**earn** and **urn**	**sole** and **soul**

A. Each sentence below has two homophones in parentheses. Use the context of the sentence to decide which is correct. Circle the correct homophone. Use a dictionary if necessary.

1. Larry's horse has a beautiful brown (main, mane).

2. The rich man lived in a beautiful (manor, manner).

3. The (night, knight) gave his loyalty to his king and fought for him.

4. The film was in a tangled mess on the (reel, real).

5. Dave was taught that it isn't right to (steel, steal) from others.

6. My sister let out a (wail, whale) when she got her finger caught in the door.

7. The (sole, soul) of my shoe is worn thin.

8. You need to (earn, urn) a lot of money in order to buy a house.

9. My dad loves to (great, grate) cheese for his homemade pizza.

10. The miners dug the (ore, or) from deep in the earth.

11. My teacher says I should be able to figure out the (main, mane) idea.

12. My grandmother was buried and a funeral (earn, urn) was placed on her grave.

13. The (wail, whale) is actually a mammal because it breathes air.

14. He has an unusual (manor, manner) of constantly interrupting people.

15. Okay, are you going (ore, or) are you staying?

Unit 10, Lesson 2

Part 3: Shades of Meaning

Words may have small differences in meaning. A reader must know the exact meaning of a word to understand what the writer is saying. For example, a joke that is *bad* is different from a joke that it is *horrible. Horrible* is much worse than bad.

A. Read the sentence with the missing word. Then read the question about the missing word. Choose the word that best answers the question.

1. The cowboy tried to_____ the rope around the wild horse.

   Which of these words would indicate that the cowboy tried to tighten the rope?

   A. stretch
   B. wrap
   C. cinch
   D. throw

2. Lou told me to "make like a tree and leave," but I thought his _____ was stupid.

   Which of these words would indicate that Lou told a play on words?

   A. idea
   B. pun
   C. story
   D. joke

3. When the huge wave hit the boat, it became _____.

   Which of these words would indicate that boat turned upside down?

   A. sunk
   B. wet
   C. swamped
   D. inverted

4. My aunt collects _____ of old clothes and sews them into blankets and quilts.

   Which of these words would indicate that the aunt collects parts left over?

   A. remnants
   B. bundles
   C. lots
   D. material

Copyright © McDougal Littell Inc.

Power Words

Look at the words below. Circle any that you think you may know. Be ready to tell the class what the word means. Also tell the class how you think you know that word.

cinch	manner	poverty	sole
feat	manor	pun	suite
flair	muddle	rap	urn
grate	ore	recuperation	view
inverted	pauper	remnants	wail
knight	poll	shudder	wealth

Part 1: Middle English Words

You've learned that many of our words come from Middle English and other languages. A dictionary tells you a word's **etymology** or origin. The etymology is given at the very end of the definition. To save space, dictionaries use letters to show the different languages. For example, M means *middle,* O means *old,* ME means *Middle English,* OFr. means *Old French,* Lat. means *Latin.* Dictionaries also use the < symbol to mean one comes from another. Look at the example below for the word *liberty.*

[ME *liberte* < OFr. < Lat. *libertas* < *liber,* free.]

You read these symbols as follows: The word *liberty* comes from the Middle English word *liberte,* which comes from the Old French, which comes from the Latin word *libertas,* which comes from the Latin word *liber,* which means "free".

A. Rewrite the following three dictionary etymologies into plain English. Use the example above as a model. Remember to use the words "which comes from" for the symbol <.

1. [ME welthe < wele < OE wela.]

   The word wealth comes from _____

   _____

2. [ME poverte < OFr. < Lat. paupertas < pauper, poor.]

   The word poverty comes from _____

   _____

3. [ME < OFr. manoir, to dwell, manor < Lat. manere, to remain.]

   The word manor comes from_____

   _____

Part 2: Homophones

Words that sound the same but have different spellings and meanings are called **homophones.** For example, **role** and **roll** are homophones.

A. In the blank provided, write a homophone for each of the words below. Look back at Lessons 1 and 2 for help if necessary.

1. poll   _____

2. feet   _____

3. wail   _____

4. knight   _____

5. or   _____

6. flair   _____

7. sweet   _____

8. earn   _____

9. grate   _____

10. rap   _____

B. Fluency: Read the story below. There are 16 homophones in the following story; however, each of them is the wrong word. Circle the incorrect homophones and write the correct word above it. Then practice reading the story until you can read it smoothly.

The king asked Eric, the night, to guard his manner. Eric knew this was no easy

feet. He had been a guessed at the castle many times so he knew it well. He knew his

weigh around. In the mane part of the castle was a grate haul that would be hard to

defend. But Eric had a heart of steal. He always knew the write thing to do. Eric had

a flare for fighting. He was reel good at it. He also had a suite smile and a pure sole.

He would urn the king's respect ore he would dye trying.

Unit 10, Lesson 3

Part 3: Shades of Meaning

Words may have small differences in meaning. A reader must know the exact meaning of a word to understand what the writer is saying.

A. Read the sentence with the missing word. Then read the question about the missing word. Choose the word that best answers the question.

1. The high winds on the bay _____ the sailboat.

   Which of these words would indicate that sailboat turned upside down?

   A. sunk
   B. inverted
   C. wet
   D. muddled

2. Vera needed a lot of _____ after she fell down the stairs.

   Which of these words would indicate that Kim would need time for getting well?

   A. sleep
   B. vacation
   C. recuperation
   D. remnants

3. Ira will always _____ when he steps out into the cold

   Which of these words would indicate that Ira will shiver?

   A. stretch
   B. muddle
   C. snuggle
   D. shudder

4. The books were a _____ when they fell all over the floor.

   Which of these words would indicate that everything was mixed up?

   A. remnant
   B. muddle
   C. model
   D. disaster

5. The soldiers picked up the _____ of the flag after the battle.

   Which of these words would indicate that the soldiers picked up the parts left over?

   A. pun
   B. cinch
   C. remnants
   D. reeds

Part A: Middle English Words

Directions: Match the Middle English origin in Column A with its modern English word from Column B. Write the correct letter in the blank provided.

Column A

1. _____ vewe

2. _____ stel

3. _____ sawol

4. _____ rappen

5. _____ graten

6. _____ pol

7. _____ wailen

8. _____ gest

9. _____ ora

10. _____ welthe

Column B

A. ore

B. rap

C. grate

D. wail

E. view

F. poll

G. wealth

H. steel

I. soul

J. guest

Directions: Finish the following dictionary etymologies in plain English.

1. [ME *welthe* < *wele* < OE *wela*]

   The word *wealth* _____

   _____

2. [ME *poverte* < OFr. < Lat. *paupertas* < *pauper*, poor.]

   The word *poverty* _____

   _____

3. [ME < OFr. *manoir*, to dwell, manor < Lat. *manere*, to remain.]

   The word *manor* _____

   _____

Unit 10, Test

Part B: Homophones

Directions: Fill in the letter of the word that is a homophone of the **bold** word

1. **feet**
   - Ⓐ fete
   - Ⓑ fate
   - Ⓒ feat
   - Ⓓ fet
   - Ⓔ fit

2. **great**
   - Ⓕ grate
   - Ⓖ grat
   - Ⓗ gret
   - Ⓘ grit
   - Ⓙ grunt

3. **flair**
   - Ⓚ flour
   - Ⓛ flow
   - Ⓜ floor
   - Ⓝ fire
   - Ⓞ flare

4. **or**
   - Ⓟ orb
   - Ⓠ hour
   - Ⓡ our
   - Ⓢ ore
   - Ⓣ out

5. **poll**
   - Ⓐ pull
   - Ⓑ pole
   - Ⓒ pool
   - Ⓓ put
   - Ⓔ pelt

6. **rap**
   - Ⓕ raid
   - Ⓖ rat
   - Ⓗ rope
   - Ⓘ wrap
   - Ⓙ where

7. **sole**
   - Ⓚ sold
   - Ⓛ soul
   - Ⓜ sun
   - Ⓝ some
   - Ⓞ sore

8. **sweet**
   - Ⓟ swede
   - Ⓠ suit
   - Ⓡ sweat
   - Ⓢ sure
   - Ⓣ suite

9. **earn**
   - Ⓐ ear
   - Ⓑ your
   - Ⓒ urn
   - Ⓓ url
   - Ⓔ whirl

10. **wail**
    - Ⓕ wait
    - Ⓖ well
    - Ⓗ weld
    - Ⓘ whale
    - Ⓙ wade

Unit 10, Test

Part C: Shades of Meaning

Read the sentence with the missing word. Then read the question about the missing word. Choose the word that best answers the question.

1. The cake became _____ when the box fell off the counter.

   Which of these words would indicate that cake turned upside down?

   A. ruined
   B. muddled
   C. inverted
   D. nasty

2. The _____ of the army straggled home after being beaten in the battle.

   Which of these words would indicate that the parts left over of the army straggled home?

   A. remnants
   B. front lines
   C. knights
   D. paupers

3. Sarah always _____ when she forgets her coat in the winter.

   Which of these words would indicate that Sarah always shivers?

   A. snuggles
   B. complains
   C. shudders
   D. cries

4. Danny needed a lot of _____ after losing the wrestling match.

   Which of these words would indicate that Danny needed time to get well?

   A. sleep
   B. recuperation
   C. wishes
   D. remnants

5. The teacher's papers were a _____ when they spilled out of her notebook.

   Which of these words would indicate that the papers were mixed up?

   A. muddle
   B. disaster
   C. remnant
   D. wonder

Power Words

Look at the words below. Circle any that you think you may know. Be ready to tell the class what the word means. Also tell the class how you think you know that word.

abnormal	benediction	compile	embolden
absent	benefit	correspond	extraordinary
arise	collapse	endanger	extraterrestrial

Part 1: Prefixes and Base Words

A **base word** is a word that can stand alone. A **prefix** is a word part added to the beginning of a base word. For example, in the word **encircle**, *circle* is the base word and *en-* is the prefix added at the beginning. Knowing the meaning of a prefix helps you figure out the meaning of the whole word. *Encircle* means "to make a circle around or surround." Study the meaning of the following prefixes until you can remember what each means.

em- and **en-** mean "in," "into," or "to make or cause" / **bene-** means "good"
a- and **ab-** mean "up," "out," "away," or "not" / **extra-** means "outside"
col-, com-, con-, and **cor-** mean "with" or "together"

A. Draw a line between the base word and the prefix for each word below. Then write what the word means on the line. Use a dictionary if necessary.

1. endanger - _____

2. arise - _____

3. correspond - _____

4. extraordinary _____

5. absent _____

6. benefit - _____

7. compile - _____

8. extraterrestrial - _____

9. collapse - _____

10. abnormal - _____

11. embolden - _____

12. benediction - _____

Unit 11, Lesson 1

Part 2: Multiple-Meaning Words

The word *multiple* means many. **Multiple-meaning** words are words that have more than one meaning. For example, the word *trip* can mean a journey. It can also be to stumble and fall down.

A. Read each sentence below. Think about how the **bold** word in the sentence is used. Then read the different meanings of that word below. Write the letter of the definition in the blank that matches the meaning of the bold word in the sentence.

_____1. The young Native American saw the **high** sails of the ship approaching.
   a. being at or near the top; extending upward
   b. having a bad smell
   c. filled with a drug

_____2. Afraid, he ran for **cover** deep into the woods.
   a. to place something over something to protect or hide it
   b. to be responsible for guarding or protecting another person
   c. something that provides shelter or protection

_____3. The explorers from another land sent out a search **party**.
   a. a social gathering
   b. a political organization
   c. a group involved in a similar activity

_____4. They captured the young man and took him to their **ship**.
   a. a vessel or large boat
   b. to send to a distant place

_____5. The explorers treated him as if he were some **kind** of animal.
   a. nice; warm-hearted
   b. a type or particular variety

_____6. The young man saw many different cities, animals, and **plants**.
   a. an organism that grows in the earth
   b. a factory where things are manufactured

_____7. He was forced to **wear** strange clothing.
   a. to run down or cause to fall apart
   b. to put on clothes

_____8. The young man was smart however, and he learned to speak their **tongue**.
   a. the fleshy organ within the mouth
   b. a flame
   c. a spoken language or dialect

Part 3: Syllabication

A **syllable** is a word part with one vowel sound. Remember that the vowels are the letters *a, e, i, o, u,* and sometimes *y.* All other letters are consonants. If you break an unknown word into syllables, it may help you figure out what the word means. Look at the rules below to see the correct places to divide words into syllables.

1. *war • plane* (between two words of a compound word)
2. *dis • arm* or *try • ing* (between a base word and a prefix or suffix)
3. *cor • rect* (between double consonants)
4. *clus • ter* (between two consonants, with vowels both before and after)
5. *be • hind* (<u>before</u> a single consonant if the vowel before it has a <u>long</u> sound)
6. *nev • er* (<u>after</u> a single consonant if the vowel before it has a <u>short</u> sound)
7. *trou • ble* (in words ending with a consonant + *-le,* divide the word before the consonant before the *-le*)

A. Use the rules above to divide each of the words below into its syllables. Write the syllables on the blanks provided. Then write which rule tells you how to divide a word.

Word		Syllables		Rule
1. friendly	=	_____	+ _____	_____
2. because	=	_____	+ _____	_____
3. hidden	=	_____	+ _____	_____
4. captive	=	_____	+ _____	_____
5. enough	=	_____	+ _____	_____
6. footprints	=	_____	+ _____	_____
7. savage	=	_____	+ _____	_____
8. coldness	=	_____	+ _____	_____
9. people	=	_____	+ _____	_____
10. native	=	_____	+ _____	_____

Power Words

Look at the words below. Circle any that you think you may know. Be ready to tell the class what the word means. Also tell the class how you think you know that word.

attendance	elegance	heroism	patriotism
brightness	fatherhood	neighborhood	resistance
convenience	fondness	patience	terrorism

Part 1: Suffixes and Base Words

A **suffix** is a word part added to the end of a word. A suffix can help you determine a word's part of speech. You remember that a noun is the name of a person, place, or thing. When you add the suffix **ness** to the adjective *kind,* it becomes the noun *kindness.* Study the following suffixes. Each suffix can turn a word or word part into a noun.

-ance as in appear<u>ance</u> / **-ence** as in differ<u>ence</u> /
-ism as in rac<u>ism</u> / **-hood** as in neighbor<u>hood</u> / **-ness** as in good<u>ness</u>

A. Draw a line between the base word and the prefix for each word below. Then write what the word means on the line. Use a dictionary if necessary.

1. attendance - _____

2. neighborhood - _____

3. patriotism - _____

4. fondness - _____

5. convenience - _____

6. elegance - _____

7. fatherhood - _____

8. terrorism - _____

9. brightness - _____

10. resistance - _____

11. patience - _____

12. heroism - _____

Unit 11, Lesson 2

Part 2: Multiple-Meaning Words

The word *multiple* means many. **Multiple-meaning** words are words that have more than one meaning. For example, the word *trip* can mean a journey. It can also be to stumble and fall down.

A. Read each sentence below. Think about how the **bold** word in the sentence is used. Then read the different meanings of that word below. Write the letter of the definition in the blank that matches the meaning of the bold word in the sentence.

_____1. The first submarine was made of wood with iron **bands** wrapped around it.
    a. muscical groups
    b. a strip of material used to encircle and hold an object together
    c. wedding rings

_____2. It was shaped like a barrel so that it would not **roll** over.
    a. to beat a drum in a continuous manner
    b. to turn over and over
    c. a small piece of bread

_____3. The submarine was just large enough for one man to **fit** inside.
    a. in good physical condition
    b. to insert or adjust so as to be properly in place
    c. a sudden outburst of emotion

_____4. When the **order** was given, the first submarine sailed towards a British ship.
    a. an arrangement of things in a certain manner
    b. food requested at a restaurant
    c. a command to do something

_____5. The sailor in the submarine hoped to **strike** a ship just below the water line.
    a. to come into forceful contact
    b. a work stoppage over a disagreement between workers and employers

_____6. Once he picked his **spot**, the sailor would prepare to blow up the ship.
    a. a particular place or location
    b. to locate a target

_____7. The sailor would begin to **drill** a hole into the ship.
    a. the training of soldiers in marching and arms
    b. to make a hole in a hard material with a drill

_____8. Once the hole was made, the sailor would **stick** a torpedo or explosives inside.
    a. a long slender piece of wood
    b. to put, thrust, or push

Unit 11, Lesson 2

Part 3: Syllabication

A **syllable** is a word part with one vowel sound. Remember that the vowels are the letters *a, e, i, o, u,* and sometimes *y.* All other letters are consonants. If you break an unknown word into syllables, it may help you figure out what the word means. Look at the rules below to see the correct places to divide words into syllables.

1. *war • plane* (between two words of a compound word)
2. *dis • arm* or *try • ing* (between a base word and a prefix or suffix)
3. *cor • rect* (between double consonants)
4. *clus • ter* (between two consonants, with vowels both before and after)
5. *be • hind* (<u>before</u> a single consonant if the vowel before it has a <u>long</u> sound)
6. *nev • er* (<u>after</u> a single consonant if the vowel before it has a <u>short</u> sound)
7. *trou • ble* (in words ending with a consonant + *-le,* divide the word before the consonant before the *-le*)

A. Use the rules above to divide each of the words below into its syllables. Write the syllables on the blanks provided. Then write which rule tells you how to divide a word.

Word		Syllables		Rule
1. success	=	_____	+ _____	_____
2. warship	=	_____	+ _____	_____
3. rifle	=	_____	+ _____	_____
4. fighting	=	_____	+ _____	_____
5. British	=	_____	+ _____	_____
6. order	=	_____	+ _____	_____
7. bullet	=	_____	+ _____	_____
8. turtle	=	_____	+ _____	_____
9. idea	=	_____	+ _____	_____
10. powder	=	_____	+ _____	_____

Copyright © McDougal Littell Inc.

Power Words

Look at the words below. Circle any that you think you may know. Be ready to tell the class what the word means. Also tell the class how you think you know that word.

abnormal	brightness	endanger	heroism
absent	collapse	embolden	neighborhood
arise	compile	extraordinary	patience
attendance	convenience	extraterrestrial	patriotism
benediction	correspond	fatherhood	resistance
benefit	elegance	fondness	terrorism

Part 1: Affixes and Base Words

A **base word** is a word that can stand alone. An **affix** is a word part added to the beginning or ending of a base word. Prefixes and suffixes are affixes. Study the meaning of the following affixes until you can remember what each means.

em- and **en-** mean "in" or "into" or "to make or cause" / **bene-** means "good"
a- and **ab-** mean "up" or "out" or "away" or "not" / **extra-** means "outside"
col-, com-, con-, and **cor-** mean "with" or "together"
-ance as in appear<u>ance</u> / **-ence** as in differ<u>ence</u> /
-ism as in rac<u>ism</u> / **-hood** as in neighbor<u>hood</u> / **-ness** as in good<u>ness</u>

A. Match the word in **Column A** with its meaning in **Column B**. Write the correct letter in the blank provided. Use a dictionary if necessary.

Column A

1. _____ endanger
2. _____ patriotism
3. _____ correspond
4. _____ convenience
5. _____ absent
6. _____ fatherhood
7. _____ compile
8. _____ extraterrestrial
9. _____ benefit
10. _____ resistance

Column B

A. the state of being a father to children

B. an advantage or aid

C. not present; missing

D. to gather together

E. a love of country or homeland

F. from outside the Earth's atmosphere

G. to communicate by letter

H. something that increases one's comfort

I. to bring into danger

J. the act of struggling against something

Part 2: Multiple-Meaning Words

The word *multiple* means many. **Multiple-meaning words** are words that have more than one meaning. For example, the word *trip* can mean a journey. It can also be to stumble and fall down.

A. Read each sentence below. Think about how the **bold** word in the sentence is used. Then read the different meanings of that word below. Write the letter of the definition in the blank that matches the meaning of the bold word in the sentence.

_____1. My dad had to wait a long time for his **order** at the fancy restaurant.
    a. an arrangement of things in a certain manner
    b. food requested at a restaurant
    c. a command to do something

_____2. We tried to **cover** ourselves from the driving rain.
    a. something that provides shelter or protection
    b. to be responsible for guarding or protecting another person
    c. to place something over something to protect or hide it

_____3. The soldiers would **drill** for four hours everyday before the parade.
    a. to make a hole in a hard material with a drill
    b. a machine that makes holes in hard materials
    c. the training of soldiers in marching and arms

_____4. Rene wanted to **ship** her presents back to her family in France.
    a. a vessel or large boat
    b. to send to a distant place

_____5. Most of the players on our baseball team are very **fit**.
    a. to insert or adjust so as to be properly in place
    b. a sudden outburst of emotion
    c. in good physical condition

B. Fluency: Practice reading the paragraph below until you can read it smoothly. Circle those words you have studied that have more than one meaning.

    My uncle is a kind person. He decided to have a party for me. At first he couldn't decide on a spot. He wanted to have it somewhere that was covered in plants. I told him my friends could fit in anywhere. He finally picked a restaurant and went to order the food. The prices were very high. A roll costs one dollar! He said "that roll better taste good on your tongue." He also paid to have two bands play. I asked him why two groups. He said, "Well, that's in case one goes on strike."

Name _____   Date _____

Part 3: Syllabication

A **syllable** is a word part with one vowel sound. Remember that the vowels are the letters *a, e, i, o, u,* and sometimes *y.* All other letters are consonants. If you break an unknown word into syllables, it may help you figure out what the word means. Look at the rules below to see the correct places to divide words into syllables.

1. *war • plane* (between two words of a compound word)
2. *dis • arm* or *try • ing* (between a base word and a prefix or suffix)
3. *cor • rect* (between double consonants)
4. *clus • ter* (between two consonants, with vowels both before and after)
5. *be • hind* (<u>before</u> a single consonant if the vowel before it has a <u>long</u> sound)
6. *nev • er* (<u>after</u> a single consonant if the vowel before it has a <u>short</u> sound)
7. *trou • ble* (in words ending with a consonant + *-le,* divide the word before the consonant before the *-le*)

A. Use the rules above to divide each of the words below into its syllables. Write the syllables on the blanks provided. Then write which rule tells you how to divide a word.

Word		Syllables		Rule
1. mammoth	=	_____ +	_____	_____
2. plunder	=	_____ +	_____	_____
3. wagon	=	_____ +	_____	_____
4. unpack	=	_____ +	_____	_____
5. table	=	_____ +	_____	_____
6. pigtails	=	_____ +	_____	_____
7. bacon	=	_____ +	_____	_____
8. huddle	=	_____ +	_____	_____
9. finish	=	_____ +	_____	_____
10. fireplace	=	_____ +	_____	_____

Name _____   Date _____

Part A: Affixes and Base Words

Directions: Match the word in **Column A** with its definition in **Column B**. Write the letter of the correct definition in the blank provided.

Column A

1. _____ patriotism
2. _____ attendance
3. _____ correspond
4. _____ collapse
5. _____ endanger
6. _____ resistance
7. _____ absent
8. _____ fondness
9. _____ fatherhood
10. _____ extraordinary
11. _____ compile
12. _____ convenience
13. _____ extraterrestrial
14. _____ abnormal
15. _____ benefit

Column B

A. the state of being a father to children

B. to fall down in one piece

C. an advantage or aid

D. a liking for something

E. not present; missing

F. not normal

G. to gather together

H. the number of persons who are present

I. a love of country or homeland

J. to put into danger

K. from outside the Earth's atmosphere

L. the act of struggling against something

M. to communicate by letter

N. beyond the ordinary

O. something that increases one's comfort

Directions: The following words have been divided both correctly and incorrectly into their affixes and base words. Write the letter of the correctly divided word on the blank.

1. _____   A. hero / ism   B. her / oism
2. _____   A. brigh / tness   B. bright / ness
3. _____   A. bene / fit   B. ben / efit
4. _____   A. ari / se   B. a / rise

Unit 11. Test

Part B: Multiple-Meaning Words

Directions: Read each sentence below. Find the word that fits in both sentences.

1. The _____ played especially well last night.

   He got so mad he took off his wedding _____.

   ○ party
   ○ cover
   ○ group
   ○ band

2. The man was speaking in a _____ I had never heard.

   The _____ of the flames reached the roof.

   ○ language
   ○ tongue
   ○ heat
   ○ order

3. My mother has a way with _____.

   The car _____ in the Midwest make a lot of cars.

   ○ bands
   ○ orders
   ○ plants
   ○ makers

4. John's family boarded the _____ for their cruise.

   Hawaii will _____ fresh pineapples to the mainland.

   ○ ship
   ○ party
   ○ plane
   ○ fly

5. When the firecracker went off, I ran for _____.

   The _____ over the bus stop wasn't big enough to keep out the rain.

   ○ order
   ○ spot
   ○ cover
   ○ safety

Unit 11, Test

Part C: Syllabication

Directions: Separate the following words into syllables. Write the syllables on the lines.

1. footprints   =   _____ + _____

2. hidden   =   _____ + _____

3. neighborhood   =   _____ + _____ + _____

4. absent   =   _____ + _____

5. captive   =   _____ + _____

6. benefit   =   _____ + _____ + _____

7. bullet   =   _____ + _____

8. rifle   =   _____ + _____

9. finish   =   _____ + _____

10. brightness   =   _____ + _____

11. plunder   =   _____ + _____

12. collapse   =   _____ + _____

13. compile   =   _____ + _____

14. fondness   =   _____ + _____

15. turtle   =   _____ + _____

16. native   =   _____ + _____

17. attendance   =   _____ + _____ + _____

18. fireplace   =   _____ + _____

19. powder   =   _____ + _____

20. abnormal   =   _____ + _____ + _____

Power Words

Look at the words below. Circle any that you think you may know. Be ready to tell the class what the word means. Also tell the class how you think you know that word.

aerobics	endure	prolong	technical
befriend	foreshadow	secure	threaten
despair	panorama	skeptical	tolerant

Part 1: Greek and Latin Roots

Many English words are made up of word parts from other languages, especially Greek and Latin. These word parts are called **roots**. A root cannot stand alone, but knowing its meaning helps you figure out the meaning of the whole word. A group of words with the same root is called a **word family**. Study the chart of **Greek** roots below.

Root	Meaning	Example
pan	all, entire	<u>pan</u>orama
techn	art, skill	<u>techn</u>ical
aero	air	<u>aero</u>bics, <u>aero</u>ate
scop, skept	look at, examine	micro<u>scop</u>e, <u>skept</u>ical
anthropo	human	<u>anthropo</u>logy

A. Match the word in **Column A** with its correct meaning in **Column B.** Write the letter of the correct meaning in the space provided. Use a dictionary if necessary.

Column A

1. _____ aerate

2. _____ technical

3. _____ microscope

4. _____ anthropology

5. _____ skeptical

6. _____ panorama

7. _____ aerobics

Column B

A. related to a mechanical or scientific skill

B. an unbroken view of a large area

C. to supply with air

D. hard exercise for raising the heart beat

E. a device for seeing very small things

F. the study of the development of humans

G. doubting what one sees or hears

Part 2: Context Clues

Remember that you can often figure out the meaning of an unknown word from the words that appear near by. The words or phrases that surround an unknown word are called **context clues**. For example, see how the ideas in the two sentences below tell you that *elated* means very happy.

Jean was elated over winning the prize. She was incredibly happy.

A. Use context clues to figure out the meaning of the **bold** word. Darken in the circle with the correct definition.

1. Anne Frank grew up in a **tolerant** city where people respected each other's beliefs.
   - ○ hateful
   - ○ respectful
   - ○ prejudiced
   - ○ old

2. When times got bad in Germany in 1930, people were afraid and did not feel **secure**.
   - ○ safe
   - ○ respectful
   - ○ nice
   - ○ angry

3. Adolf Hitler became the leader of German, and he began to **threaten** people he didn't like, such as Jews.
   - ○ defend
   - ○ respect
   - ○ terrorize
   - ○ protect

4. Hitler sent people he didn't like to concentration camps to be **tortured** and killed.
   - ○ talked to
   - ○ supported
   - ○ hurt
   - ○ fed

5. At first, Anne's family tried to **endure** their hardships and live a normal life.
   - ○ run from
   - ○ talk about
   - ○ escape
   - ○ withstand

6. As things got worse, the family felt **despair** and ran away to a city in another country.
   - ○ hope
   - ○ delight
   - ○ hopelessness
   - ○ confident

Unit 12, Lesson 1

Part 3: Prefixes and Base Words

A **base word** is a word that can stand alone. A **prefix** is a word part added to the beginning of a base word. For example, in the word **self-doubt**, *doubt* is the base word and *self-* is the prefix added at the beginning. Knowing the meaning of a prefix helps you figure out the meaning of the whole word. *Self-doubt* means "to doubt or lose faith in one's abilities." Study the meaning of the following prefixes until you can remember what each means.

self- means "oneself" or "automatic" / **be-** means "cause to become" or "about"
pro- means "forward" / **ex-** means "out" or "former"
fore- means "before" or "earlier"

A. Draw a line between the base word and the prefix for each word below. Then write what the word means on the line. Use a dictionary if necessary.

1. progress - _____

2. express - _____

3. forewarn - _____

4. beloved - _____

5. self-control - _____

6. prolong - _____

7. befriend - _____

8. self-defense - _____

9. expatriate - _____

10. foresee - _____

11. beware - _____

12. self-esteem - _____

13. propel - _____

14. bemoan - _____

15. foreshadow - _____

Power Words

Look at the words below. Circle any that you think you may know. Be ready to tell the class what the word means. Also tell the class how you think you know that word.

academic	encounter	innermost	revolutionary
childish	gradual	obedient	transfer
disintegrate	heroic	resentment	variety

Part 1: Greek and Latin Roots

Many English words are made up of word parts from other languages, especially Greek and Latin. These word parts are called **roots.** A root cannot stand alone, but knowing its meaning helps you figure out the meaning of the whole word. A group of words with the same root is called a **word family.** Study the chart of **Latin** roots below.

Root	Meaning	Example
grad	step, stage	graduate, gradual
fer	carry, bear	transfer, ferry
var	different	variety, vary
pon, pos, posit	place, put	deposit, position
capt, cept	take, have	capture, accept

A. Match the word in **Column A** with its correct meaning in **Column B.** Write the letter of the correct meaning in the space provided. Use a dictionary if necessary.

Column A

1. _____ variety
2. _____ graduate
3. _____ deposit
4. _____ transfer
5. _____ accept
6. _____ position
7. _____ gradual

Column B

A. to receive or take something willingly

B. to give for safekeeping, such as money

C. a place or location

D. having many different types or forms

E. to carry from one place to another

F. to move forward in regular stages

G. to be granted an academic degree

Unit 12, Lesson 2

Part 2: Context Clues

Remember that you can often figure out the meaning of an unknown word from the words that appear near by. The words or phrases that surround an unknown word are called **context clues**. For example, see how the ideas in the two sentences below tell you that *infuriated* means very mad.

Jack was infuriated over losing the game. He screamed angry words at everyone.

A. Use context clues to figure out the meaning of the **bold** word. Darken in the circle with the correct definition.

1. When Admiral Byrd went to Antarctica alone, he did not **encounter** any other people.
   ○ travel with
   ○ pay
   ○ meet
   ○ know

2. Byrd had to be **obedient** to the laws of nature, doing whatever nature told him to do.
   ○ disrespectful
   ○ obeying
   ○ nice
   ○ wishful

3. In the severe cold, the weather could turn bad and **disintegrate** in a matter of minutes.
   ○ improve
   ○ rain
   ○ become fair
   ○ fall apart

4. At one point, Byrd became deathly sick and had **nausea** in his stomach for days.
   ○ sickness
   ○ food
   ○ cold
   ○ worms

5. One day, Byrd stumbled and dropped his flashlight into a deep **crevasse** in the ice.
   ○ well
   ○ crack
   ○ forest
   ○ cliff

6. It was so cold in Antarctica that the sun seemed barely able to **hoist** itself in the sky.
   ○ shine
   ○ raise
   ○ lower
   ○ sink

Name _____   Date _____

Part 3: Suffixes and Base Words

A **base word** is a word that can stand alone. A **suffix** is a word part added to the end of a base word. For example, in the word **excitement**, *excite* is the base word and *-ment* is the suffix added at the end. Knowing the meaning of a suffix helps you figure out the meaning of the whole word. *Excitement* means "the state of being excited." Study the meaning of the following suffixes until you can remember what each means.

-ary means "relating to" or "about" / **-most** means "at the extreme"
-ish means "characteristic of" / **-ic** means "relating to" / **-ment** means "state of"

A. Draw a line between the base word and the suffix for each word below. Then write what the word means on the line. Use a dictionary if necessary.

1. topmost - _____

2. Spanish - _____

3. microscopic - _____

4. requirement - _____

5. legendary - _____

6. childish - _____

7. contentment - _____

8. heroic - _____

9. selfish - _____

10. revolutionary - _____

11. innermost - _____

12. resentment - _____

13. imaginary - _____

14. foolish - _____

15. academic - _____

Power Words Review

Look at the words below. Circle any that you think you may know. Be ready to tell the class what the word means. Also tell the class how you think you know that word.

academic	encounter	obedient	skeptical
aerobics	endure	panorama	technical
befriend	foreshadow	prolong	threaten
childish	gradual	resentment	tolerant
despair	heroic	revolutionary	transfer
disintegrate	innermost	secure	variety

Part 1: Greek and Latin Roots

Many English words are made up of word parts from other languages, especially Greek and Latin. Study the chart of **Greek** and **Latin** roots below. Then do the exercise on the next page.

Root	Meaning	Example
pan	all, entire	panorama
techn	art, skill	technical
aero	air	aerobics, aerate
scop, skept	look at, examine	microscope, skeptical
anthropo	human	anthropology
grad	step, stage	graduate. gradual
fer	carry, bear	transfer, ferry
var	different	variety, vary
pon, pos, posit	place, put	deposit, position
capt, cept	take, have	capture, accept

Unit 12, Lesson 3

Part 1: Greek and Latin Roots continued

A. Match the word with its correct meaning.

1. _____ aerate   A. to receive or take something willingly

2. _____ variety   B. to move forward in regular stages

3. _____ microscope   C. to supply with air

4. _____ panorama   D. to give for safekeeping, such as money

5. _____ skeptical   E. a device for seeing very small things

6. _____ deposit   F. having many different types or forms

7. _____ transfer   G. doubting what one sees or hears

8. _____ gradual   H. to carry from one place to another

9. _____ technical   I. an unbroken view of a large area

10. _____ accept   J. related to a mechanical or scientific skill

Part 2: Context Clues

A. Underline the context clues, or definitions, for the **bold** words in the sentences.

1. Jack felt sad and terrible, in **despair**, that his dog had died.

2. We were surprised to **encounter**, or meet, Lois at the store.

3. We watched our team's leading score **disintegrate**. It slowly disappeared.

4. Stupid people try to **threaten**, or terrorize, others to get them to do something.

5. Juan is always **obedient** to his mother. He does whatever she asks him to do.

6. I feel very **secure** in our neighborhood. We live in a safe part of town.

7. My friends are very **tolerant**. They accept many different types of people.

8. One should never **torture** little animals. It is wrong to capture and hurt something.

9. It is hard for me to **endure** winter. I cannot withstand the cold very well.

10. David fell into the **crevasse** on the mountain. He slipped at the edge of the crack.

Unit 12, Lesson 3

Part 3: Affixes and Base Words

A **base word** is a word that can stand alone. An **affix** is a word part added to the beginning or end of a base word. Prefixes and suffixes are affixes. Study the meaning of the following affixes until you can remember what each means.

self- means "oneself" or "automatic" / **be-** mean "cause to become" or "about"
pro- means "forward" / **ex-** means "out" or "former"
fore- means "before" or "earlier"
-ary means "relating to" or "about" / **-most** means "at the extreme"
-ish means "characteristic of" / **-ic** means "relating to" / **-ment** means "state of"

A. Draw a line between the base word and the affix for each word below. Then write what the word means on the line. Use a dictionary if necessary.

1. befriend - _____

2. childish - _____

3. foreshadow - _____

4. heroic - _____

5. self-control - _____

6. prolong - _____

7. innermost - _____

8. academic - _____

9. expatriate - _____

10. resentment - _____

B. Fluency: Practice reading the following paragraph until you can read it smoothly. The underlined words have affixes. Draw a line between the affix and the base word.

It was <u>foolish</u> for me to be mad at my friend. I could <u>bemoan</u> the fact that he yelled at me. I could keep my <u>resentment</u>. I could let it affect my <u>self-esteem</u>. In other words, I could be <u>childish</u>. However, I did not want to <u>prolong</u> these bad feelings any longer. Instead I decided to let go of my <u>imaginary</u> anger. The next time I saw him I would <u>express</u> my <u>innermost</u> thoughts. Such an act is not <u>heroic</u>. It is what one has to do to find <u>contentment</u>. It is a <u>requirement</u> of being friends.

Part A: Greek and Latin Roots

Directions: Match the meaning of the word in **Column B** with the word in **Column A**. Fill in the letter of the definition on the blank provided.

Column A

1. _____ microscope
2. _____ deposit
3. _____ aerate
4. _____ accept
5. _____ anthropology
6. _____ position
7. _____ panorama
8. _____ variety
9. _____ gradual
10. _____ aerobics
11. _____ skeptical
12. _____ transfer
13. _____ technical
14. _____ graduate

Column B

A. to receive or take something willingly

B. an unbroken view of a large area

C. to give for safekeeping, such as money

D. related to a mechanical or scientific skill

E. a place or location

F. hard exercise for raising the heart beat

G having many different types or forms

H. a device for seeing very small things

I. to carry from one place to another

J. the study of the development of humans

K. to move forward in regular stages

L. doubting what one sees or hears

M. to be granted an academic degree

N. to supply with air

Directions: Each Latin and Greek root below has two definitions. Only one is correct. Write the letter of the correct one on the blank provided.

1. _____ techn   A. carry, bear   B. art, skill

2. _____ var   A. different   B. air

3. _____ scop, skept   A. look at, examine   B. place, put

4. _____ fer   A. carry, bear   B. human

5. _____ aero   A. different   B. air

6. _____ pon, pos, posit   A. place, put   B. take, have

Unit 12, Test

Part B: Context Clues

Directions: For each numbered blank, there is a list of words with the same number. Choose the word from each list that best completes the meaning of the paragraph.

1. Harry was very _____. He would do what his mother said even when he was

    (1)

    in _____ and felt sad and hopeless.

    (2)

1.		2.	
○ childish		○ good spirits
○ skeptical		○ despair
○ obedient		○ panorama
○ lazy		○ joy

2. Sean tried to _____ Adam to get him to do what he wanted. Sean would

    (3)

    terrorize Adam, but Adam was strong and would withstand or _____ Sean.

    (4)

3.		4.	
○ encounter		○ despair
○ threaten		○ tolerant
○ befriend		○ endure
○ prolong		○ aerate

3. Jose felt very _____. Everyone he met or _____ in the new school treated

    (5)   (6)

    him with respect.

5.		6.	
○ secure		○ endured
○ threatened		○ secured
○ scared		○ encountered
○ obedient		○ ran from

4. We live in a _____ town. Even when things begin to fall apart, or _____,

    (7)   (8)

    people continue to respect others who are different.

7.		8.	
○ childish		○ disintegrate
○ technical		○ endure
○ skeptical		○ foreshadow
○ tolerant		○ secure

Unit 12, Test

Part C: Prefixes and Suffixes

Directions: Fill in the letter of the word that most nearly matches the meaning of the underlined word.

1. to <u>express</u>
   - Ⓐ sleep
   - Ⓑ say
   - Ⓒ lie
   - Ⓓ walk
   - Ⓔ dream

2. to <u>befriend</u>
   - Ⓕ lie
   - Ⓖ try out
   - Ⓗ make enemies
   - Ⓘ refuse
   - Ⓙ make friends

3. the students <u>bemoan</u>
   - Ⓚ sing
   - Ⓛ talk
   - Ⓜ wish
   - Ⓝ complain
   - Ⓞ sleep

4. a <u>childish</u> man
   - Ⓟ boring
   - Ⓠ mature
   - Ⓡ kind
   - Ⓢ mean
   - Ⓣ immature

5. a <u>microscopic</u> piece
   - Ⓐ tiny
   - Ⓑ costly
   - Ⓒ in bad shape
   - Ⓓ able to catch fire
   - Ⓔ dirty

6. an <u>imaginary</u> tale
   - Ⓕ true
   - Ⓖ silly
   - Ⓗ made-up
   - Ⓘ long
   - Ⓙ stupid

7. a <u>revolutionary</u> act
   - Ⓚ old
   - Ⓛ extreme
   - Ⓜ wise
   - Ⓝ timely
   - Ⓞ repeated

8. to <u>prolong</u> the class
   - Ⓟ watch
   - Ⓠ lengthen
   - Ⓡ cancel
   - Ⓢ love
   - Ⓣ hate

9. <u>innermost</u> thoughts
   - Ⓐ most private
   - Ⓑ most public
   - Ⓒ stupidest
   - Ⓓ wisest
   - Ⓔ most annoying

10. a <u>heroic</u> boy
    - Ⓕ happy
    - Ⓖ slow
    - Ⓗ brave
    - Ⓘ tired
    - Ⓙ lazy

Unit 1, Lesson 1

Part 1: Multiple Meaning Words

A.
1. a
2. b
3. b
4. a
5. b
6. b

Part 2: Idioms

A.
1. c
2. a
3. b
4. d

B.
1. E
2. A
3. C
4. H
5. D
6. I
7. F
8. J
9. G
10. B

Part 3: Context Clues

A.
1. cook
2. worry
3. duty
4. baked dessert
5. warm

Unit 1, Lesson 2

Part 1: Multiple Meaning Words

A.
1. b
2. a
3. a
4. a
5. b
6. a
7. a

Part 2: Idioms

A.
1. E
2. I
3. K
4. H
5. G
6. L
7. A
8. B
9. J
10. F
11. D
12. C

Part 3: Context Clues

A.
1. tired
2. told in secret
3. small piece
4. new or unusual happening
5. complicated or complex

Unit 1, Lesson 3

Part 1: Multiple Meaning Words

A.
1. a
2. b
3. b
4. b
5. a
6. b

Part 2: Idioms

A.
1. J
2. F
3. I
4. D
5. E
6. C
7. A
8. B
9. G
10. H

B.
1. bugging me
2. birdbrain
3. give me your ear
4. hightail it
5. stay in touch
6. busy as a bee
7. second wind
8. put her nose to the grindstone
9. all thumbs
10. sink or swim
11. got the hang of it
12. walking on air
13. a straight face

Part 3: Context Clues

A.
1. new or unusual happening
2. baked dessert
3. told in secret
4. worry or fear
5. complicated or complex
6. small piece

Unit 1, Unit Test

Part A: Multiple Meaning Words

1. film
2. rake
3. tracks
4. broke
5. profile

Part B: Idioms

1. O
2. A
3. M
4. B
5. J
6. I
7. N
8. C
9. K
10. E
11. L
12. G
13. D
14. H
15. F

Part C: Context Clues

1. chef
2. morsel
3. confided
4. fatigued
5. obligation
6. hearty
7. envolved
8. anxiety

Unit 2, Lesson 1

Part 1: Prefixes and Base Words

A.
1. anti/freeze – a liquid that prevents other liquids from freezing
2. in/capable – not able to do something
3. mal/formed – made or formed badly
4. anti/aircraft – weapons used to destroy aircraft
5. il/literate – not able to read
6. im/mortal – living forever
7. anti/terrorism – against terrorism
8. mal/treat – to treat badly
9. im/mobile – not able to move
10. anti/social – one who doesn't enjoy the company of others
11. il/legal – not lawful
12. mal/nourish – badly fed or nourished

Part 2: Idioms

A.
1. b.
2. d
3. a.
4. c.

B.
1. J
2. I
3. C
4. G
5. D
6. B
7. F
8. H
9. A
10. E

Part 3: Specialized Vocabulary

A.
1. a baseball field
2. a hit that sails over the outfield fence
3. the part without the grass nearest the batter
4. to swing and miss a pitch
5. the player between second and third base
6. the spot in front of the catcher facing the pitcher
7. ball that is hit up in the air
8. the small hill from which the pitcher throws the ball

Unit 2, Lesson 2

Part 1: Prefixes and Base Words

A.
1. multiparty – a political system having more than one party
2. hypercritic – one who is extremely critical
3. monogamy – the belief in having a relationship with one person at a time
4. omnidirectional – in all directions
5. multilingual – able to speak more than one language
6. hypertension – high blood pressure

Part 2: Idioms

A.
1. J
2. B
3. E
4. K
5. A
6. D
7. I

8. C
9. L
10. H
11. F
12. M
13. G
14. N

Part 3: Specialized Vocabulary

A.
1. one who leads musicians
2. the musical apparatus played by a musician
3. the stick with which a conductor uses to show the orchestra the rhythm
4. the part of an orchestra made up of instruments that use stretched strings to make sound, such as the violins, violas, etc.
5. a large group of musicians playing multiple instruments who play together
6. the part of an orchestra made up of horns, such as trumpets, tubas, etc.
7. a thin slice of bamboo that vibrates when a musician blows across it
8. any musical instrument on which the player hits or beats to make a sound

Unit 2, Lesson 3

Part 1: Prefixes and Base Words

A.
1. hyper/critical – extremely critical
2. in/capable – not able to do something
3. mal/formed – badly formed or made
4. monogamy – a belief in being in a relationship with one person at a time
5. il/literate – not able to read
6. multi-lingual – able to speak more than one langue
7. anti/terrorism – something or someone that works against terrorism
8. mal/treat – to treat badly
9. im/possible – not possible
10. omni/directional – in all directions

Part 2: Idioms

A.
1. F
2. C
3. I
4. A
5. J
6. G
7. B
8. H
9. D
10. E

B.
1. in the thick
2. took cover
3. heart sank
4. get this straight
5. dead against
6. paid a red price
7. taking its toll
8. black as pitch
9. work up the nerve
10. combed
11. high and low
12. stay put
13. blood would run cold
14. a dream come true
15. rang out the news

Part 3: Specialized Vocabulary

A.
1. ball
2. shortstop
3. infield
4. mound
5. homeplate
6. diamond

Unit 2, Unit Test

Part A: Prefixes and Based Words

1. O
2. H
3. B
4. M
5. L
6. C
7. E
8. I
9. A
10. N
11. D
12. J
13. F
14. G
15. K

1. A
2. A
3. A
4. B
5. A

Part B: Idioms

1. O
2. C
3. L
4. M
5. K
6. B
7. D
8. A
9. J
10. H
11. E
12. G
13. N
14. F
15. I

Part C: Specialized Vocabulary

Category A: Baseball

diamond	infield	fly ball
mound	home plate	shortstop
homer	strikes	

Category B: Music

percussion	conductor	string instruments
orchestra	reed	baton
brass section	instrument	

Unit 3, Lesson 1

Part 1: Context Clues

A.
1. set plan
2. needed
3. mad and impatient
4. tease

Part 2: Synonyms

A.
1. practice
2. holy
3. dreamy
4. laughter
5. arguments
6. rude comments

Part 3: Compound Words

A.
1. repairman
2. roadblock
3. strawberry
4. sunrise
5. undergrowth

B.
1. strawberry
2. sunrise
3. roadblock
4. undergrowth
5. repairman
6. undergrowth
7. strawberries
8. sunrise
9. repairman
10. roadblock

Unit 3, Lesson 2

Part 1: Context Clues

A.
1. beat
2. part of a meal
3. column
4. put out

Part 2: Synonyms

A.
1. steal
2. pull
3. hot
4. assassin
5. race
6. quit
7. mob
8. last
9. hurry
10. increase
11. nap
12. cried
13. full
14. part
15. tool

Part 3: Hyphenated Compound Words

A. 1. self respect
    2. fly fishing
    3. father in law
    4. reel to reel
    5. pinch hit
    6. butter fly   short lived
    7. air planes   fly over
    8. grand father   steel trap
    9. trade in   dish washer

Unit 3, Lesson 3

Part 1: Context Clues

A. 1. mad and impatient
    2. columns
    3. beat
    4. tease

Part 2: Synonyms

A. 1. O   9. B
    2. F   10. K
    3. J   11. A
    4. N   12. C
    5. M   13. D
    6. G   14. I
    7. L   15. E
    8. H

Part 3: Compound Words

A. 1. repair/man – one who fixes things
    2. road/block – something to stop traffic
    3. under/growth – low plants growing below other plants
    4. sun/rise – dawn
    5. self/respect – a feeling of confidence and caring about oneself
    6. base/ball – a round object used in the game of the same name
    7. dish/washer – a machine that washes dishes and utensils
    8. grand/father – the father of one's father
    9. air/plane – a vehicle that flies through the air
    10. trade/in – something given at a store in order to get a discounted price

B. 1. father-in-law   8. assassin
    2. disgusted   9. custom
    3. repairman   10. annoy
    4. system   11. disputes
    5. short-lived   12. self-respect
    6. roadblock   13. trade-in
    7. mob   14. hilarity

Unit 3, Unit Test

Part A: Context Clues

1. disgusted
2. course
3. pulse
4. extinguished
5. system
6. pillar
7. annoy
8. required

Part B: Synonyms

1. b
2. j
3. m
4. s
5. d
6. i
7. n
8. p
9. c
10. g

Part C: Compound Words

1. O
2. I
3. B
4. L
5. N
6. K
7. F
8. D
9. A
10. H
11. M
12. J
13. E
14. G
15. C

1. B
2. B
3. B
4. A

Unit 4, Lesson 1

Part 1: Prefixes and Base Words

A.
1. post/graduate – related to an advanced degree after high school or college
2. semi/pro – taking part in a sport in a part-time basis
3. co/worker – a colleague
4. de/fog – to remove humidity or fog
5. post/operative – after a surgical operation
6. co/operate – to work together
7. semi/soft – not completely hard
8. co/exist – to live together peacefully
9. de/rail – to leave the tracks on a railroad, to knock off course
10. semi/circle – a half circle
11. co/sign – to sign a document with others
12. semi/annual – twice a year

Part 2: Context Clues

A.
1. kind
2. the person who gets another's money and title
3. someone pretending to be someone else
4. sent away
5. behavior
6. sickness

Part 3: Homophones

A.
1. steak
2. route
3. hear
4. tide
5. see
6. plane
7. here
8. root
9. paws
10. tow

B.
1. stake – a stick stuck into the ground: steak – a cut of beef
2. it's – contraction for it is: tail – the appendage on the end of an animal
3. plane – an aircraft: plain – a large flat surface of land

Unit 4, Lesson 2

Part 1: Suffixes and Base Words

A.
1. along the length of something
2. very clean
3. full of cheer or happiness
4. with courage
5. full of truth or honesty
6. all the time

Part 2: Context Clues

A.
1. stay in
2. sadly
3. remember
4. wanderer
5. place to mine stone
6. flexible

Part 3: Homophones

A.
1. in – into: inn – a hotel or motel
2. daze – confusion: days – a twenty-four hour period
3. be – to exist: bee – an insect with a stinger
4. flee – to run away: flea – an insect that lives on animals
5. him – a male person: hymn – a religious song
6. fur – hair on an animal: fir – a type of tree
7. find – to discover something: fined – to pay a penalty
8. prays – to meditate or converse with a higher power: praise – good comments
9. tense – nervous: tents: a cloth structure for sleeping out of doors
10. peer – to look closely: pier – a wooden structure that extends into water

Unit 4, Lesson 3

Part 1: Affixes and Base Words

A.
1. F
2. G
3. D
4. H
5. C
6. I
7. A
8. J
9. B
10. E

Part 2: Context Clues

A.
1. sent away
2. flexible
3. behavior
4. remember
5. sickness
6. stay in

Part 3: Homophones

A.
1. daze
2. fined
3. pier
4. stake
5. sea
6. inn
7. tents
8. tide
9. root
10. tow
11. fir
12. flea

B.
1. flea – flee
2. plain – plane
3. see – sea
4. root – route
5. here – hear
6. inn – in
7. tied – tide
8. daze – days
9. tents – tense
10. him – hymn
11. peer – pier
12. bee – be
13. toe – tow
14. fined – find
15. its – it's
16. stake – steak

Unit 4, Unit Test

Part A: Affixes and Base Words

1. M
2. I
3. O
4. J
5. D
6. C
7. N
8. L
9. A
10. B
11. F
12. G
13. H
14. E
15. K

1. B
2. A
3. B
4. B
5. B

Part B: Context Clues

1. nomad
2. banished
3. affliction
4. recollect
5. impostor
6. heir
7. adaptable
8. occupy

Part C: Homophones

1. d
2. j
3. m
4. q
5. b
6. j
7. m
8. p
9. d
10. h

Unit 5, Lesson 1

Part 1: Antonyms

A.
1. seriously
2. empty
3. frown
4. falling
5. dull

Part 2: Latin Roots

A.
1. K
2. D
3. J
4. G
5. C
6. H
7. B
8. A
9. F
10. E

Part 3: Shades of Meaning

A.
1. C
2. A
3. D
4. B

Unit 5, Lesson 2

Part 1: Antonyms

A.
1. loved
2. danger
3. artificial
4. sour
5. still

Part 2: Latin Roots

A.
1. G
2. D
3. H
4. A
5. E
6. C
7. K
8. J
9. B
10. C

Part 3: Shades of Meaning

A.
1. C
2. B
3. D
4. B

Unit 5, Lesson 3

Part 1: Antonyms

A.
1. D
2. H
3. E
4. I
5. J
6. F
7. B
8. A
9. C
10. G

Part 2: Latin Roots

A. 1. E
    2. G
    3. A
    4. H
    5. C
    6. D
    7. B
    8. F

Part 3: Shades of Meaning

A. 1. C
    2. A
    3. C
    4. D

Unit 5, Unit Test

Part A: Antonyms

1. c
2. f
3. o
4. q
5. d
6. i
7. m
8. p
9. a
10. i

Part B: Latin Roots

1. M
2. J
3. L
4. B
5. N
6. O
7. K
8. C
9. E
10. H
11. D
12. G
13. I
14. F
15. A

1. A
2. A
3. B
4. A

Part C: Shades of Meaning

1. D
2. B
3. C
4. A

Unit 6, Lesson 1

Part 1: Context Clues

A. 1. evil
    2. idiot
    3. stupid
    4. fooled

Part 2: Multiple Meaning Words

A. 1. b
    2. b
    3. b
    4. c
    5. a
    6. b
    7. b
    8. a

Part 3: Prefixes and Base Words

A. 1. counter/argument – an argument against another's opionion
    2. over/see – to match over; to direct
    3. contra/band – materials illegally shipped to somewhere
    4. mid/day – noon or the middle of the day
    5. circuí/navigate – to travel around something
    6. overspend – to spend more than a set amount
    7. counter/claim – to claim or have an opinion different to another's
    8. circum/ference – the distance around a circle
    9. mid/summer – in the middle of the summer
    10. contra/dict – to correct or say the opposite of another
    11. mid/town – in the middle of downtown

Unit 6, Lesson 2

Part 1: Context Clues

A. 1. broke apart
    2. countryside
    3. without people
    4. friends

Part 2: Multiple Meaning Words

A. 1. b
    2. b
    3. a
    4. b
    5. a
    6. c
    7. a
    8. b

Part 3: Prefixes and Base Words

A. 1. up/ward – towards the ceiling or sky
2. strength/en – to become stronger
3. sea/worthy – safe for sailing on the sea or ocean
4. lady/like – gracious, in the manner of a cultured lady
5. skyward – toward the sky
6. beaut/ician – one who makes others more beautiful; hairdresser
7. length/en – to become longer
8. trust/worthy – safe to be trusted
9. war/like – looking or acting like war
10. mus/ician – a person who plays music
11. quick/en – to become quicker or faster
12. home/ward – to go towards one's home

Unit 6, Lesson 3

Part 1: Context Clues

A. 1. friends
2. idiot
3. countryside
4. without people

Part 2: Multiple Meaning Words

A. 1. b   5. a
2. a   6. a
3. c   7. b
4. b   8. b

Part 3: Prefixes and Base Words

A. 1. H   9. N
2. F   10. O
3. I   11. E
4. J   12. D
5. K   13. B
6. M   14. C
7. A   15. G
8. L

Unit 6, Unit Test

Part A: Context Clues

1 comrade
2. sinister
3. imbecile
4. idiotic
5. uninhabited
6. terrain
7. deluded
8. disintegrate

Part B: Multiple Meaning Words

1. cross
2. growth
3. button
4. serve
5. open

Part C: Affixes and Base Words

1. F
2. A
3. H
4. C
5. I
6. J
7. B
8. E
9. G
10. D

1. F
2. H
3. G
4. B
5. A
6. D
7. E
8. C

Unit 7, Lesson 1

Part 1: Structural Analysis

A.
1. un/break/able – not able to be broken
2. un/earth/ly – not of this earth or real
3. re/place/able – able to be placed again or copied
4. pre/print/ed – was printed before
5. re/wire/d – to have been wired once again
6. un/love/ly – ugly; not pretty
7. pre/soak/ed – has been soaked before washing

Part 2: Syllabication

A.
1. B   5. B
2. B   6. B
3. B   7. A
4. A   8. A

Part 3: Context Clues

A.
1. necessary
2. not to trust
3. open space
4. happy
5. brutal persons
6. men chosen to fight each other in front of others in ancient times
7. wild and powerful
8. wanting to get one's way

Unit 7, Lesson 2

Part 1: Structural Analysis

A.
1. mal/adjust/ed – one who doesn't fit in well with others
2. dis/please/d – was not pleased or happy with something
3. multi/task/ing – doing many tasks or jobs at once
4. dis/place/r – one who moves others around
5. multi/color/ed – had many colors
6. mal/form/ed – was badly formed
7. dis/approv/ing – not approving of something

Part 2: Syllabication

A.
1. A
2. A
3. B
4. B
5. B

B.
1. mis/take   6. per/son
2. in/no/cent   7. foot/steps
3. put/ting   8. quick/ly
4. ti/ger   9. eye/lids
5. a/part   10. wo/man

Part 3: Context Clues

A.
1. ten years
2. breakfast dish of eggs filled with other ingredients
3. artist's workroom
4. jewelry that pins to one chest
5. cost to go to school
6. skillful
7. extra amount
8. inspect

Unit 7, Lesson 3

Part 1: Structural Analysis

A.
1. H   5. A
2. F   6. D
3. G   7. B
4. E   8. C

Part 2: Syllabication

A.
1. 1
2. 5
3. 6
4. 3
5. 2
6. 4

Part 3: Context Clues

A.
1. untrustingly
2. fighter
3. needed
4. costs
5. extra amount
6. inspect

Unit 7, Unit Test

Part A: Structural Analysis

1.
2. F
3. C
4. N
5. J
6. L
7. B
8. D
9. M
10. G
11. H
12. E
13. A
14. K

Part B: Syllabication

1. lum + py
2. rab + bit
3. un + friend + ly
4. hun + ger
5. fin + ish
6. home + made
7. wo + man
8. pow + er + ful
9. ca + ble
10. in + no + cent
11. pet + al
12. a + part
13. de + fense + less
14. mis + take
15. foot + steps
16. in + tent + ly
17. cork + screw
18. bright + ly
19. suf + fer
20. air + plane

Part C: Context Clues

1. barbarians
2. clearing
3. willful
4. tuition
5. decade
6. studio
7. savage
8. gladiators

Unit 8, Lesson 1

Part 1: Specialized Vocabulary

A.
1. Roman galley – an early wooden ship powered by a large number of soldiers or slaves
2. oars – wooden paddles
3. Chinese junk – a light, flat-bottomed ship with large sails
4. sails – large pieces of cloth to catch the wind
5. rudder – steering bar
6. deck – top surface of a ship
7. Clipper – wooden ship had two to four masts that held large sails; the ship went very fast
8. masts – long wooden poles that held large sails
9. steamship – a ship with an engine powered by boiling water, or steam
10. paddle-wheel boat – a steamship pushed by a large wheel of flat boards that revolved down into the water to push the ship forward
11. tanker – a modern, metal ship with an empty inside which is filled with oil
12. hulls – sides and bottoms of ships

Part 2: Using a Dictionary

A.
1. noun – a platform that goes from one side of a ship to another
2. noun – the dry outer covering of a seed, fruit, or nut
3. verb – to make boxing motions as if to hit someone
4. verb – to guide a vehicle or vessel
5. noun – the frame or body of a ship

Part 3: Greek and Latin Roots

A.
1.	F	6.	D
2.	A	7.	H
3.	E	8.	C
4.	J	9.	I
5.	B	10.	G

Unit 8, Lesson 2

Part 1: Specialized Vocabulary

A. 1. crust – the thin outer layer of the earth
    2. earthquake – a shaking of the earth's surface caused by quick movement of the earth's crust
    3. faults – places where giant sections of the earth's crust meet
    4. epicenter – the place below the earth's surface where the earthquake originates
    5. seismologists – people who study earthquakes
    6. tsunamis – large sea waves caused by earthquakes

Part 2: Using a Dictionary

A. 1. noun – the hard outer layer of bread
    2. idiom – to be guilty or in error
    3. noun – a ride or swell moving through the surface of a body of water
    4. verb – to move freely up and down or back and forth, as branches in the wind
    5. noun – a weakness in one's personality or character

Part 3: Greek and Latin Roots

A. 1. J   6. C
    2. G   7. B
    3. A   8. E
    4. I   9. D
    5. H   10. F

Unit 8, Lesson 3

Part 1: Specialized Vocabulary

A. 1. D   4. C
    2. E   5. B
    3. A

Part 2: Using a Dictionary

A. 1. D   9. L
    2. M   10. N
    3. H   11. F
    4. C   12. I
    5. K   13. E
    6. B   14. J
    7. O   15. G
    8. A

Part 3: Greek and Latin Roots

A. 1. F   5. B
    2. A   6. D
    3. E   7. H
    4. G   8. C

Unit 8, Unit Test

Part A: Specialized Vocabulary

Ships	Earthquakes
clipper	epicenter
tanker	seismologists
hull	fault
steamship	crust
rudder	tsunamis
deck	
junk	

1. C
2. F
3. H
4. G
5. D
6. B
7. A
8. E

Part B: Using a Dictionary

1. noun – the frame or body of a ship
2. noun – the outer layer of the earth's surface
3. noun – a wooden or metal pole used to support a sail on a boat
4. noun – a platform that goes form one side of a ship to another
5. verb – to guide a vehicle or vessel

Part C: Greek and Latin Roots

1. D
2. E
3. L
4. F
5. I
6. B
7. C
8. G
9. H
10. K
11. A
12. J

1. A
2. B
3. B
4. B
5. B
6. A
7. A
8. B

Unit 9, Lesson 1

Part 1: Greek and Latin Roots

A. 1. B
    2. C
    3. D
    4. E
    5. F
    6. A

Part 2: Multiple-Meaning Words

A. 1. b   5. b
    2. c   6. b
    3. a   7. c
    4. c   8. b

Part 3: Syllabication

A. 1. de + fy   4
    2. hum + ble   7
    3. ap + pren + tice   5 and 3
    4. moon + light   1
    5. un + lock   2
    6. ad + vis + ers   6 and 2

Unit 9, Lesson 2

Part 1: Greek and Latin Roots

A. 1. E
    2. D
    3. F
    4. B
    5. C
    6. A

Part 2: Multiple-Meaning Words

A. 1. b   5. c
    2. b   6. d
    3. b   7. b
    4. b   8. a

Part 3: Syllabication

A. 1. ap + prove   5
    2. ter + ri + ble   5 and 7
    3. mo + tion + less   4 and 2
    4. pig + tails   1
    5. of + fend   5
    6. un + fair   2

Unit 9, Lesson 3

Part 1: Greek and Latin Roots

A. 1. J   7. H
    2. G   8. D
    3. I   9. B
    4. L   10. F
    5. K   11. C
    6. A   12. E

Part 2: Multiple-Meaning Words

A. 1. flight   7. bow
    2. party   8. ear
    3. deep   9. maid
    4. pack   10. cross
    5. scales   11. leave
    6. check   12. break

Part 3: Syllabication

A. 1. moon + light   1
    2. un + lock   2
    3. of + fend   5
    4. hum + ble   7
    5. de + fy   4
    6. mo + tion + less   4 and 2
    7. ap + prove   5
    8. ap + pren + tice   5 and 3
    9. pig + tails   1
    10. ter + ri + ble   5 and 7

Unit 9, Unit Test

Part A: Greek and Latin Roots

1. L
2. C
3. B
4. J
5. A
6. K
7. E
8. D
9. I
10. F
11. G
12. H

1. A
2. A
3. B
4. A
5. B
6. B
7. B
8. B

Part B: Multiple-Meaning Words

1. pass
2. flight
3. party
4. cross
5. scales

Part C: Syllabication

1. moon + light
2. un + lock
3. ter + ri + ble
4. si + lence
5. ap + prove
6. mo + tion + less
7. pig + tails
8. de + fy
9. un + fair
10. quick + ly
11. ap + pren + tice
12. of + fend
13. peo + ple
14. base + ball
15. hum + ble
16. clus + ters
17. ad + vis + ers
18. nev + er
19. ca + ble
20. war + plane

Unit 10, Lesson 1

Part 1: Middle English Words

A.
1. I
2. A
3. K
4. B
5. G
6. C
7. L
8. J
9. F
10. D
11. E
12. H

Part 2: Homophones

A.
1. wrap
2. flare
3. feet
4. right
5. reed
6. hall
7. guessed
8. guest
9. poll
10. bred

B.
1. way – weigh
2. we've – weave
3. died – dyed
4. missed – mist
5. sweet – suite

Part 3: Shades of Meaning

A.
1. shudder
2. recuperation
3. reeds
4. muddle

Unit 10, Lesson 2

Part 1: Middle English Words

A.
1. L
2. D
3. A
4. H
5. I
6. B
7. E
8. G
9. K
10. F
11. C
12. J

Part 2: Homophones

A.
1. mane
2. manor
3. knight
4. reel
5. steal
6. wail
7. sole
8. earn
9. grate
10. ore
11. main
12. urn
13. whale
14. manner
15. or

Part 3: Shades of Meaning

A.
1. cinch
2. pun
3. inverted
4. remnants+

Unit 10, Lesson 3

Part 1: Middle English Words

A. 1. The word *wealth* comes from the Middle English word *welthe*, which comes from the word *wele*, which comes from the Old Engish word *wela*.
   2. The word *poverty* comes from the Middle English word *poverte*, which comes from the Old French, which comes from the Latin word *paupertas*, which comes from the word *pauper*, which means "poor."
   3. The word *manor* comes from Middle English, which comes from the Old French word *manoir*, which means "to dwell" or "manor," which comes from the Latin word *manere*, which means "to remain."

Part 2: Homophones

A. 1. pole   6. flare
   2. feat   7. suite
   3. whale   8. urn
   4. night   9. great
   5. ore   10. wrap

B. 1. night – knight
   2. manner – manor
   3. feet – feat
   4. guessed – guest
   5. weigh – way
   6. mane – main
   7. grate – great
   8. haul – hall
   9. steal – steel
   10. write – right
   11. flare – flair
   12. reel – real
   13. suite – sweet
   14. sole – soul
   15. urn – earn
   16. dye – die

Part 3: Shades of Meaning

A. 1. inverted
   2. recuperation
   3. shudder
   4. muddle
   5. remnants

Unit 10, Unit Test

Part A: Middle English Words

1. E
2. H
3. I
4. B
5. C
6. F
7. D
8. J
9. A
10. G

1. The word *wealth* comes from the Middle English word *welthe*, which comes from the word *wele*, which comes from the Old Engish word *wela*.
2. The word *poverty* comes from the Middle English word *poverte*, which comes from the Old French, which comes from the Latin word *paupertas*, which comes from the word *pauper*, which means "poor."
3. The word *manor* comes from Middle English, which comes from the Old French word *manoir*, which means "to dwell" or "manor," which comes from the Latin word *manere*, which means "to remain."

Part B: Homophones

1. c
2. f
3. o
4. s
5. b
6. i
7. l
8. t
9. c
10. i

Part C: Shades of Meaning

1. inverted
2. remnants
3. shudders
4. recuperation
5. muddle

Unit 11, Lesson 1

Part 1: Prefixes and Base Words

A. 1. en/danger – to put into danger
    2. a/rise – to get up; to raise up
    3. cor/respond – to communicate by letter; to be in agreement; conformity
    4. extra/ordinary – beyond the normal or ordinary
    5. ab/sent – not present; missing
    6. bene/fit – an advantage or aid
    7. com/pile – to gather together
    8. extra/terrestrial – from outside the Earth's atmosphere
    9. col/lapse – to fall down in one piece
   10. ab/normal – not normal
   11. em/bolden – to make bold or give courage
   12. bene/diction – a blessing or prayer

Part 2: Multiple-Meaning Words

A. 1. a
    2. c
    3. c
    4. a
    5. b
    6. a
    7. b
    8. c

Part 3: Syllabication

A. 1. friend + ly   2
    2. be + cause   5
    3. hid + den   3
    4. cap + tive   4
    5. e + nough   5
    6. foot + prints   1
    7. sav + age   6
    8. cold + ness   2
    9. peo + ple   7
   10. na + tive   5

Unit 11, Lesson 2

Part 1: Suffixes and Base Words

A. 1. attend/ance – the number of persons who are present
    2. neighbor/hood – the area surrounding one's home
    3. patriot/ism – a love of country or homeland
    4. fond/ness – a liking for something
    5. conveni/ence – something that increases one's comfort
    6. eleg/ance – having a rich and fine quality
    7. father/hood – the state of being a father
    8. terror/ism – the unlawful use of force to intimidate a government
    9. bright/ness – having an abundance of light
   10. resist/ance – the act of struggling against something
   11. pati/ence – the capacity to endure hardship without complaint
   12. hero/ism – heroic conduct; courage

Part 2: Multiple-Meaning Words

A. 1. b
    2. b
    3. b
    4. c
    5. a
    6. a
    7. b
    8. b

Part 3: Syllabication

A. 1. suc + cess   3
    2. war + ship   1
    3. ri + fle   5 or 7
    4. fight + ing   2
    5. Brit + ish   6
    6. or + der   4
    7. bul + let   3
    8. tur + tle   7
    9. i + de + a   5
   10. pow + der   4

Unit 11, Lesson 3

Part 1: Affixes and Base Words

A.
1. I
2. E
3. G
4. H
5. C
6. A
7. D
8. F
9. B
10. J

Part 2: Multiple-Meaning Words

A.
1. b
2. c
3. a
4. b
5. c

B.
1. kind	7. order
2. party	8. high
3. spot	9. roll
4. covered	10. tongue
5. plants	11. bands
6. fit	12. strike

Part 3: Syllabication

A.
1. mam + moth	3
2. plun + der	4
3. wag + on	6
4. un + pack	2
5. ta + ble	5 or 7
6. pig + tails	1
7. ba + con	5
8. hud + dle	3 or 7
9. fin + ish	6
10. fire + place	1

Unit 11, Unit Test

Part A: Affixes and Base Words

1. I
2. H
3. M
4. B
5. J
6. L
7. E
8. D
9. A
10. N
11. G
12. O
13. K
14. F
15. C

1. A
2. B
3. A
4. B

Part B: Multiple-Meaning Words

1. band
2. tongue
3. plants
4. ship
5. cover

Part C: Syllabication

1. foot + prints
2. hid + den
3. neigh + bor + hood
4. ab + sent
5. cap + tive
6. ben + e + fit
7. bul + let
8. ri + fle
9. fin + ish
10. bright + ness
11. plun + der
12. col + lapse
13. com + pile
14. fond + ness
15. tur + tle
16. na + tive
17. at + tend + ance
18. fire + place
19. pow + der
20. ab + nor + mal

Unit 12, Lesson 1

Part 1: Greek and Latin Roots

A.
1. C
2. A
3. E
4. F
5. G
6. B
7. D

Part 2: Context Clues

A.
1. respectful
2. safe
3. terrorize
4. hurt
5. withstand
6. hopelessness

Part 3: Prefixes and Base Words

A.
1. pro/gress – movement toward a goal
2. ex/press – to say something; something that moves quickly
3. fore/warn – to warn ahead of time
4. be/loved – someone loved
5. self/control – to control one's emotions and actions
6. pro/long – to extend the time of an event
7. be/friend – to make a friend of someone
8. self/defense – to protect oneself
9. ex/patriate – someone who lives outside of their native country
10. fore/see – to know something will happen ahead of time
11. self-esteem – confidence or self-respect
12. be/ware – to be on guard or cautious of something
13. pro/pel – to push or thrust forward
14. be/moan – to complain
15. fore/shadow – to give a hint of what will happen

Unit 12, Lesson 2

Part 1: Greek and Latin Roots

A.
1. D
2. G
3. B
4. E
5. A
6. C
7. F

Part 2: Context Clues

A.
1. meet
2. obeying
3. fall apart
4. sickness
5. crack
6. raise

Part 3: Suffixes and Base Words

A.
1. top/most – the highest in order, rank, or position
2. Span/ish – related to the country of Spain
3. microscop/ic – very small
4. require/ment – something that is necessary
5. legend/ary – famous; well-known
6. child/ish – immature; behaving like a child
7. content/ment – a state of being satisfied; happy
8. hero/ic – extremely brave or selfless
9. self/ish – concerned totally with oneself
10. revolution/ary – something extreme or very new
11. inner/most – the deepest or most private
12. resent/ment – ill will as a result of something someone has done
13. imagin/ary – unreal
14. fool/ish – stupid; lacking good judgment
15. academ/ic – related to education or school

Unit 12, Lesson 3

Part 1: Greek and Latin Roots

A.
1. C
2. F
3. E
4. I
5. G
6. D
7. H
8. B
9. J
10. A

Part 2: Context Clues

A.
1. felt sad and terrible
2. meet
3. slowly disappeared
4. terrorize
5. does whatever she asks him to do
6. safe
7. accept many different types of people
8. capture and hurt
9. withstand
10. crack

Part 3: Affixes and Base Words

A.
1. be/friend – to make a friend of someone
2. child/ish – immature; behaving like a child
3. fore/shadow – to hint at something that will happen
4. hero/ic – very brave or selfless
5. self/control – to control one's emotions and behavior
6. pro/long – to extend the time of an event
7. inner/most – the deepest or most private
8. academ/ic – related to education or school
9. ex/patriate – someone who lives outside of their native country
10. resent/ment – ill will at something someone has done

B.
1. fool/ish
2. be/moan
3. resent/ment
4. self/esteem
5. child/ish
6. pro/long
7. imagin/ary
8. ex/press
9. inner/most
10. hero/ic
11. content/ment
12. require/ment

Unit 12, Unit Test

Part 1: Greek and Latin Roots

1. H
2. C
3. N
4. A
5. J
6. E
7. B
8. G
9. K
10. F
11. L
12. I
13. D
14. M

1. B
2. A
3. A
4. A
5. B
6. A

Part 2: Context Clues

1. obedient
2. despair
3. threaten
4. endure
5. secure
6. encountered
7. tolerant
8. disintegrate

Part 3: Prefixes and Suffixes

1. b
2. j
3. n
4. t
5. a
6. h
7. l
8. q
9. a
10. h

Greek and Latin Roots Used In PowerWords

aero means "air"

anthrop means "human"

aud means "hear"

auto means "self, alone"

bibl and *biblio* mean "books"

bio means "life"

capt and *cept* mean "take, have"

cardi means "heart"

cede, ceed, and *cess* mean "go, yield, give away"

chron means "time"

cycl means "circle, ring"

dem means "people"

dic or *dict* mean "speak, say, tell"

div means "separate"

doc means "teach"

duc and *duct* mean "lead"

equi means "equal"

fact and *fect* mean "do, make"

flect or *flex* mean "bend"

fer means "carry, bear"

form means "form or shape"

fract and *frag* mean "break"

funct means "perform"

gen means "birth, race, kind"

geo means "earth"

grad means "step, stage"

graph and *gram* mean "write, draw, describe"

grat and *grac* mean "pleasing"

hydr means "water"

ject means "throw, hurl"

jud means "judge"

junct means "join"

liber means "free"

loc and *locat* mean "place"

log means "word, reason, study"

mech means "machine"

mem and *ment* mean "mind"

meter and *metr* mean "measure"

miss and *mit* mean "send"

mob, mot, and *mov* mean "move"

mort means "death"

Greek and Latin Roots
Used In PowerWords continued

neo means "new"

nom and *nym* mean "name, word, law"

not means "note, mark"

opt means "visible"

ortho means "straight, correct"

para means "get ready"

pel and *puls* mean "drive, thrust, urge, throb"

phil means "love"

phob means "fear"

phon means "sound"

photo means "light"

phys means "nature"

poli means "city"

pon, pos, and *posit* mean "place, put"

port means "carry"

psych means "mind, soul, spirit"

ques means "ask, seek"

rupt means "break"

schola means "school"

scop and *skept* mean "look at, examine"

scope means "see"

scrib or *script* mean "write"

sens or *sent* mean "feel"

soph means "wise"

spec, spect, and *spic* mean "look, see"

tain, ten, and *tent* mean "hold"

techn means "art, skill"

tele means "far, distant"

theo means "god"

therm means "heat"

trac and *tract* mean "pull, move"

turb means "confusion"

var means "different"

ven and *vent* mean "come"

vert or *ver* mean "turn"

voc means "voice, call"

volv means "roll"

vid or *vis* mean "see"

Homophones
Used In PowerWords

be/bee	blue/blew	no/know
here/hear	to/too/two	hi/high
new/knew	see/sea	there/they're/their
bear/bare	by/buy/bye	deer/dear
ate/eight	for/four/fore	our/hour
red/read	lead/led	meat/meet
plane/plain	rode/road/rowed	sail/sale
stare/stair	we'll/wheel	hole/whole
wear/ware/where	one/won	flower/flour
right/write	your/you're	its/it's
not/knot	gate/gait	time/thyme
son/sun	hey/hay	made/maid
male/mail	nay/neigh	oh/owe
pail/pale	peek/peak	reed/read
so/sew/sow	root/route	shone/shown
break/brake	cent/sent/scent	flee/flea
creak/creek	die/dye	fair/fare
hair/hare	heard/herd	night/knight
steel/steal	tail/tale	thrown/throne
fir/fur	waist/waste	week/weak
we've/weave	way/weigh	wait/weight
threw/through	aisle/I'll	ball/bawl
beat/beet	course/coarse	cheap/cheep
days/daze	doe/dough	heel/heal
do/dew/due	in/inn	need/knead
lone/loan	ring/wring	pole/poll
earn/urn	past/passed	sweet/suite
ore/or	rain/reign/rein	role/roll
sole/soul	seller/cellar	soar/sore
steak/stake	some/sum	tow/toe
vein/vane/vain	medal/metal	tea/tee
great/grate	poor/pour	haul/hall
piece/peace	flair/flare	mist/missed
mane/main	wail/whale	died/dyed
manor/manner	pier/peer	rap/wrap
maze/maize	air/heir	prays/praise
base/bass	wade/weighed	knave/nave
bread/bred	guessed/guest	real/reel
sees/seas	feet/feat	humn/him
scents/sense/cents	tents/tense	sight/site
fined/find	side/sighed	tide/tied
paws/pause	born/borne	chord/cord
foul/fowl	mourn/morn	

Prefixes Used in PowerWords

a- and *ab-* mean "up," "out," "away," or "not"

anti- means "against"

be- means "cause to become" or "about"

bene- means "good"

bi- means "two"

circum- means "around"

co- means "together, equally, jointly"

col-, com-, con-, and *cor-* mean "with" or "together"

contra- means "opposed" or "against"

counter- means "opposite" or "contrary"

de- means "make the opposite of"

dis- means "not" or "lack of"

em- and *en-* mean "in," "into," or "to make or cause"

ex- means "out" or "former"

extra- means "outside"

fore- means "before" or "earlier"

hyper- means "more than normal"

im-, il-, and *in-* mean "not"

inter- means "among" or "between"

intra- means "within"

ir- means "not"

mal- means "bad"

mid- means "halfway"

mis- means "wrong" or "wrongly"

mono- means "one"

multi- means "many"

non- means "not"

omni- means "all"

over- means "above" or "superior"

post- means "after" or "later"

pre- means "before"

pro- means "forward"

re- means "again" or "back"

self- means "oneself" or "automatic"

semi- means "half"

sub- means "below"

super- means "above" or "beyond"

trans- means "across"

tri- means "three"

un- means "not" or "the opposite of"

uni- means "one"

Suffixes Used in Power Words

-able/-ible means "wanting to" or "able to be"
-al means "relating to"
-ance turns a word or word part into a noun
-ant and *-ist* mean "one who does something"
-ate means "having" or "full of"
-ation, -ion, -sion, and *-ment* mean "a state or quality of"
-ence turns a word or word part into a noun
-er means "more" or "more than" (comparative)
-est means "the most" (superlative)
-fy or *-ify* means "to make"
-ful means "full of" or "having"
-hood turns a word or word part into a noun
-ise or *-ize* means "to become"
-ious/-ous means "possessing" or "full of"
-ism turns a word or word part into a noun
-less means "without" or "lacking"
-ness turns a word or word part into a noun
-some means "likely to"
-ways means "in what manner"

Rules for Syllabication

When a word is composed of two complete words (a compound word), divide between the two words.

cork • screw	fire • place	war • plane
fence • post	girl • friend	light • weight

When there are identical consonants between vowels, the word is divided between consonants.

big • ger	cor • rect	rab • bit
suf • fer	sum • mer	win • ner

Prefixes and suffixes generally form separate syllables.

dis • arm	mis • read	quick • ly
try • ing	un • do	un • friend • ly

When there is one consonant between two vowel sounds, the consonant usually goes with the second syllable, if the preceding vowel is long.

be • hind	be • lieve	de • cide
pho • to	pi • lot	si • lence

When there is one consonant between two vowel sounds, the consonant usually goes with the first syllable, if the vowel is short.

nev • er	pet • al	prof • it
mod • el	cab • in	fin • ish

Accent Generalizations

The accent usually falls on or within the root word of a word containing a prefix and/or a suffix.

    re play'   truth' ful   dis able'   cool' est

In a compound word, the primary accent usually falls on, or within, the first word.

    air' plane   fire' place   wheel' chair   up' stairs

In a two-syllable word that functions as either a noun or verb, the accent is usually on the first syllable when the word is used as a noun, and the second syllable when the word functions as a verb.

    pre' sent   pre sent'   con' tract   con tract'

When there is a double consonant within a word, the accent usually falls on the syllable which ends with the first letter of the double consonant.

    snug' gle   din' ner   mat' ter   rab' bit

In a multi-syllabic word ending in "ion" the primary accent falls on the syllable preceding the "ion" ending.

    re la' tion   ed u ca' tion

When the last syllable of a word is composed of two vowel letters, that syllable is usually accented.

    com pose'   con tain'

When there is no other clue in a two-syllable word, the accent most often falls on the first syllable.

Dolch List of Sight Words

a	did	his
about	does	hold
after	done	hot
again	don't	how
all	down	hurt
am	draw	I
an	drink	if
and	eat	in
any	eight	into
are	every	is
around	fall	it
as	far	its
ask	fast	jump
at	find	just
ate	first	keep
away	five	kind
be	fly	know
because	for	laugh
been	found	let
before	four	light
best	from	like
better	full	little
big	funny	live
black	gave	long
blue	get	look
both	give	made
bring	go	make
brown	goes	many
but	going	may
buy	good	me
by	got	much
call	green	must
came	grow	myself
can	had	never
carry	has	new
clean	have	no
cold	he	not
come	help	now
could	here	of
cut	him	off

old	six	us
on	sleep	use
once	small	
one	so	very
only	some	walk
open	soon	want
or	start	warm
our	stop	was
out	take	wash
over	tell	we
own	ten	well
pick	thank	went
play	that	were
please	the	what
pretty	their	when
pull	them	where
put	then	which
ran	there	white
read	these	who
red	they	why
ride	think	will
right	this	wish
round	those	with
run	three	work
said	to	would
saw	today	write
see	together	yellow
seven	too	yes
she	try	you
show	two	your
sing	up	
sit	upon	